The Girlfriend's Guide to Hockey

the Girlfriend's guide to HOCKEY

by teena spencer

WITH WILL FERGUSON & BRUCE SPENCER

KEY PORTER BOOKS

Canadian Cataloguing in Publication Data

Spencer, Teena
    The girlfriend's guide to hockey

ISBN 1-55263-065-X

1. Hockey.   I. Ferguson, Will.   II. Spencer, Bruce (Bruce Robert)
III. Title.

| GV847.S636 | 1999 | 796.962′024′042 | C99-931098-4 |

The publisher gratefully acknowledges the support of the Canada Council for the Arts and the Ontario Arts Council for its publishing program.

Canada

We acknowledge the financial support of the Government of Canada through the Book Publishing Industry Development Program (BPIDP) for our publishing activities.

Key Porter Books Limited
70 The Esplanade
Toronto, Ontario
Canada M5E 1R2

www.keyporter.com

Design and Electronic formatting: Lightfoot Art & Design Inc.
Image of Stanley Cup (p. 82) courtesy of Brian McFarlane

Printed and bound in Canada

99 00 01 02 03   6 5 4 3 2 1

Contents

INTRODUCTION:

Hockey in the Bedroom

Ice hockey has traditionally been a male domain—from fans to players to coaches, "a guy thing." But the last few years have seen a surprising demographic shift. More women than ever are watching—and playing—hockey. In the words of *Chatelaine* magazine, "the secret—jealously guarded by boys and men for close to a century—is out: hockey is the most fun going."

It's true, and I should know. I'm one of those newly drafted female fans.

My passion for hockey didn't light up the sky immediately. I had a healthy hatred of the game to overcome first. Newfoundland humorist Ray Guy called hockey a pestilence that was "nasty, boring, pernicious, deadening, silly, obnoxious, tedious." Televised hockey, said Guy, "turns a large proportion of the population into gibbering idiots for six months of the year." I couldn't have agreed more.

Then hockey invaded my bedroom.

When I first met Bruce, I thought I had discovered the perfect mate: sensitive, caring, artistic, sexy. He was a metalsmith like myself, he believed in equality, he even had a ponytail. We fell in love and everything was wonderful—until one fateful evening in spring.

I called Bruce and asked if he wanted to take a romantic stroll along the riverside. "I'd love to," he said. "But I can't. The playoffs are starting."

"The playoffs?"

"Montreal and New York. Opening game. Why don't you grab some beer and come over?"

I was horrified. It was like discovering your best friend was a spy for the other side. Instead of spending a quiet evening awash in romantic ambiance, we sat in his room, watching a hockey game. As Bruce yelled at the refs and knocked back the beer, I asked myself—as thousands of girlfriends and wives ask themselves every year—"What's the big deal about hockey?"

To me, the game seemed chaotic. Nothing made any sense. The referees were constantly blowing their whistles, the puck skidded along a random path, and then—for no obvious reason—a fight would break out. It looked like the stupidest sport on earth.

A few months later, Bruce asked me to marry him. Instead of simply being ecstatic, I had some reservations. One of them was a season ticket for front-row television viewing of testosterone-driven hockey players charging up and down the ice. It chilled my enthusiasm.

"Bruce," I said. "About this affection you have for hockey."

"Greatest game on earth!" he said, as if that was all the explanation needed.

I knew then I had a choice to make. Bruce would never give up hockey and I would never give up Bruce. Either I was going to spend a lot of time clenching my jaw and muttering under my breath, or I could learn something about the game. But when I set out to teach myself the basics, I was soon disappointed. There were no books that explained the rudiments of hockey in terms that an average uninitiated adult—or a woman with a mission—could understand.

But, I persisted, and after wading through dozens of bulky hockey encyclopedias, watching countless games, and faithfully reading the next days' sports pages, I slowly began to understand how hockey works. I also enlisted the help of my dear friend Will Ferguson, a writer and a hockey afficionado. Will and Bruce had been holding hockey round-table discussions (which I usually daydreamed through) since we had met. The more the three of us talked about the games we watched, the more I enjoyed and understood them. I could now spot a bad call or a delayed penalty. I could tell a clean check from a dirty one. I even understood the blue-line rule–something a lot of die-hard fans still haven't figured out. What I had been dismissing for years as a "guy thing" revealed itself as an intricate sport of strategy and speed. I never did learn to accept the fighting, but, over time, I began to enjoy the game every bit as much as did Bruce and Will.

Bruce and I are married now, and the playoffs are greatly anticipated around our house. We move the TV into the bedroom and watch the games late into the night, yelling ourselves hoarse and jumping up and down on the bed. After the game we are too excited to sleep, and since we are already in bed …

Whose bright idea was this anyway?
Where Hockey Came From and Where It's Going

You'd think the origins of hockey would be fairly well documented, but no: It's like trying to discover who invented fire. I have read all kinds of fanciful theories that place the birth of hockey in medieval England, ninth-century Denmark, seventeenth-century Scotland, and even—incredibly—in 500 B.C., when the ancient Greeks supposedly strapped animal ribs onto their sandals and skated on ponds high in the mountains. It wouldn't surprise me if some hockeyologist somewhere managed to trace hockey back to the Jurassic period: "Cave paintings in Africa depict stegosaurs playing a surprisingly familiar if rudimentary version of hockey with brontosaurs."

Hans: The Little Dutch Boy Who "Schaat"

Of the many explanations of the game I encountered, my favorite is a tale that appears in Brian McFarlane's *Hockey: The Book for Kids*. It tells the tale of young Hans, an apocryphal young lad who stumbles upon a crooked branch while skating along the frozen canals of Holland. Using the branch, he begins passing a small stone across the ice. His friends join in and—*Shazaam!*—hockey is born.

Holland is often proclaimed to be the homeland of hockey. Oil paintings by Pieter Bruegel the Elder done in 1565 depict people playing what appears to be hockey on Holland's canal ice, but this is a misinterpretation. The word skate may come from the Dutch *schaat*, but the people in the paintings are playing a variation of golf, not hockey.

Where the Game Began, and Where It Didn't

Although we may never know for sure, we can be fairly certain that hockey did *not* begin in Holland, or in Finland or Scotland. Hockey, like baseball, basketball, and football, was invented—and perfected—in the New World.

In *The Puck Starts Here*, hockey historian Garth Vaughn traces the roots of ice hockey back to a specific pond outside a boys' academy in the town of Windsor, Nova Scotia. Students at King's College were playing a game called "hurley-on-ice" as early as 1800. Hurley is an Irish field game brought to Nova Scotia by early settlers. And Long Pond, as it is known, is the birthplace of hockey.

The Canadian province of Nova Scotia gave hockey its first basic rules, wooden pucks, hockey sticks, self-fastening hockey skates, and even the box net, styled, it is said, after a fisherman's net, and first used in Halifax on January 6, 1899.

As Vaughn notes, "hockey was not invented. Rather, it grew or evolved gradually from hurley-on-ice." Still, the roots were clearly in the Maritimes. You can probably win a lot of bets on this one: hockey did not begin in Montreal, and it certainly did not begin in Kingston, Ontario. These are stubborn myths.

When hockey was first played in Montreal in 1875, the players sent to Halifax for sticks and played by "the Halifax Rules." The famous McGill Rules (the first written rules and the basis for the rules used today) were formulated by James Creighton, "the Father of Organized Hockey," who was from Halifax, Nova Scotia.

Hockey U.S.A.!

The first place to take up ice hockey outside of Nova Scotia was Boston, Massachusetts. Nova Scotia and New England have long enjoyed trade and friendship, and hockey was a natural export between the two. On November 5, 1859, the *Boston Evening Gazette* described in detail a game that was unquestionably hockey, and urged Bostonians to take it up. The editors reported that they were sending to Nova Scotia for sticks in order to introduce the sport, described as "the most exciting game that is played on the ice," to their fair city. Even today, Boston is a hockey stronghold, with a rabid, diehard cadre of fans.

"hurley"

"shinny"

"bandy"

"horky"

"hawkey"

Rule, Britannia

Hockey had crossed the Atlantic by 1863, when Queen Victoria watched her husband play a game of "ice hockey" (a term coined in Britain, apparently, to distinguish the game from field hockey). The original bouncy rubber ball was soon replaced by a wooden puck. Jolly good fun. Among the players was Albert, Prince Consort, who was in goal. Queen Victoria watched from the sidelines, and yes, she *was* amused—even though she had to leave halfway through to go give birth to a royal offspring.

What's in a Name?

The early game went by several names: wickets, rickets, hurley-on-ice, and (my personal favorite) break-shins. Every group had its own field version: in Scotland it was called "shinny" (that term is still used to describe casual pickup games, without refs or full equipment); in England it was known as "bandy," as well as "hawkey," "horkey," and "hockie." The Mi'kmaq Indians had a field-and-stick game as well, called "Oochamkunutk." But it was the Irish version, "hurley," that gave birth to ice hockey.

The word *hockey* itself is very old. Some claim that it derives from the French word *hoquet*, meaning "shepherd's staff," after the crooked shape of the early sticks. The only problem is that hockey developed first among English-speaking Canadians, and the word *hockey* was already in use long before the French began playing the game.

Colonel Hockey

An equally intriguing, and equally dubious, explanation of the origins of the name is that it is derived from a colonel stationed near Windsor, Nova Scotia, whose last name was Hockey (a common surname in that area even today). When he encouraged his troops to play hurley-on-ice during the long, harsh winters, the sport became known as "Hockey's game."

Pucks, Potatoes, and Frozen Horse Poop

What to use for a puck? Early objects included rubber balls, frozen potatoes, lumps of coal, cross-sections cut from cherry trees, and the always popular frozen horse droppings. It's just as well the early outdoor games had to end before the thaw.

Big Game

Reserved Seating

The Greatest Show on Earth

Any Date Any Time

ROW AA
SEAT 34

423A 78787

When vulcanized rubber pucks were first produced, the technique wasn't quite perfected and the pucks had a habit of breaking in two at critical moments. During one important game, the puck split on the goal-post, and only half of it went into the net. As the ref scratched his head, the opposing team cried no goal and the scoring team insisted just as adamantly that a point be awarded. A compromise was offered by a fan who yelled "Give 'em half a point!" The official finally disallowed it, saying that whatever went into the net was not regulation size.

Several years later, during the 1902 finals, the same thing happened. This time, the ref allowed the point. There was no such thing, he insisted, as "half a goal."

The Mi'kmaq Tradition

The Mi'kmaq Indians of Nova Scotia called hurley-on-ice "Alchamadijik." In this version of the game, the goalposts were at 90-degree angles to where they are today. Players had to shoot from the side, and no one could score from straight on. It made for a much more complex, tight-playing game, and for many years the Mi'kmaq version was dominant throughout Nova Scotia. But the goal line was eventually turned to face the players, a Nova Scotia net was added to catch pucks, and the flow of the game changed. Long wild shots became much more common.

The Colored League Gives Hockey Some Pizzazz

Back in the days of segregation, a separate Colored Hockey League was formed (the term "colored" was not considered a racial slur at that time). The CHL, founded in 1900 with seven teams, featured the best black players in Nova Scotia and Prince Edward Island. The level of play was high, and the league soon attracted record crowds to its games. Newspapers of the day were often patronizing, or downright hostile, to the notion of black hockey players, but the league built a solid fan base and lasted well into the 1920s.

Among the innovations the CHL introduced was a greater freedom for goaltenders. Hard to imagine, but goalies were once forced to stay on their feet during the entire game and were only allowed to kick at or poke away a puck. Goalies who fell on one to stop it were fined two dollars. The CHL allowed goalies—indeed, encouraged them—to make dramatic heart-stopping saves, falling down, sprawling out. The rest of hockey would not catch up until 1917, when other leagues began allowing their goalies to "go down" as well.

Players in Long Skirts

Hockey and women, women and hockey: The two have always gone hand-in-hand. The first organized women's hockey games began in the early 1890s, with the women playing in long woolen skirts and turtleneck sweaters. This slowed the game down a bit, but it certainly kept the players warm. And it gave the goalies a distinct advantage over their male counterparts; a long skirt is a natural puck stopper. Female goalies began letting their skirts down to ice level and secretly sewing buckshot into the hems to give added weight.

The long skirts were eventually replaced with heavy bloomers that left the women more mobile, and the Starr manufacturing company soon began marketing hockey skates specifically designed for women, called the "Lady's Beaver."

The Game Moves West

As interest in hockey expanded, every area made its own innovations. Western Canada revolutionized play in several key ways. In Winnipeg, the high-snapping wrist shot emerged and the face-off was introduced. Further west, the Pacific Coast Hockey Association (PCHA) sprouted teams in Vancouver, Victoria, New Westminster, Portland, Spokane, and Seattle. They developed their own brand of hockey as well, with distinct rules and surprising innovations. The first artificial ice in Canada was in Pacific rinks. The PCHA introduced neutral zones, penalty shots, an organized playoff system, and passing rules that helped speed up the game. (I'll explain these and other terms in Chapter 2.)

The NHL Is Born

Today, the National Hockey League (NHL) reigns supreme in professional hockey. But in the early days dozens of leagues formed and dissolved. Today's NHL actually began as a hobby for rich men. It was based in the rough mining towns of Northern Ontario and in the urban centers of Quebec and Toronto. Back then, it was called the National Hockey Association (NHA) and it was just one league of many.

The NHA became the NHL mainly because the team owners couldn't stand one of their members, a brash, abrasive man named Eddie Livingstone, who had a team in Toronto. The other owners got together and decided to oust him. They did it in a rather underhanded way—they voted to dissolve the NHA and then immediately re-formed as the NHL, this time without Livingstone. As one of the owners noted, with malicious glee, "Eddie still has his franchise. He just hasn't got a league to play in."

The Cold War on Ice

In hockey history there are only three dates to remember: 1972, 1980, and 1990.

In 1972, Team Canada played the Soviet Union in a hard-fought seven-game series that was not decided until only thirty-four seconds remained on the clock. This moment has a deep, almost religious significance for Canadians. Most can remember exactly where they were when Paul Henderson scored his famous goal. You'd think they'd won the Cold War or something.

And it's not just men who had epiphanies at that moment. Julie Stevens, co-author of *Too Many Men on the Ice*, watched Henderson's winning goal on television when she was in elementary school and she vividly recalls the children running outside, cheering and shouting. It was the same energy she felt eighteen years later, in 1990, when Canada came from behind to win the gold at the first official Women's World Ice Hockey Championship. It's moments like these that burn themselves into your memory and turn you into a fan.

For Americans, the Magical Moment came, not in 1972 or 1990, but on February 22, 1980, at the Winter Olympics at Lake Placid, when an ABC sportscaster exclaimed: "Do you believe in miracles? Yes!"

It was dubbed the "Miracle on Ice." The U.S. Olympic Hockey team surprised the Soviet Union's team (and the rest of the world) with an amazing 4–3 upset. Key to the U.S. team's win was the amazing goaltending powers of Jim Craig. When Team U.S.A. finally earned their gold in the last round of the Olympics, in a tough game against Finland, Craig was at center stage. In one of hockey history's most touching episodes, Craig skated slowly around the arena, an American flag draped over his shoulders, looking for his father in the stands.

After their win, Team U.S.A. was treated to a heroes' welcome. They visited the White House and made appearances all over the country.

In Search of the Elusive Hockey Metaphor

Karen Byne, a player with the U.S. national women's hockey team, used to wear a t-shirt that read: "Hockey is life. The rest is just details."

There is something about hockey that inspires heady metaphors and fanciful symbolism. Canadians seem more prone to this than Americans, and at times it can get downright silly. Here is a small sampling.

In *Pride & Glory*, sportswriter William Houston describes the Significance of Hockey this way:

> Hockey, in many ways, defines the Canadian soul. If Americans champion freedom of the individual and entrepreneurship, Canadians, living in a cold and often harsh climate, deal in the collective, of working together for a common goal.

So you can see there is a lot more to this than a bunch of grown men chasing a frozen piece of rubber around the ice. I mean, we're talking *soul*. In *Home Game*, goaltender Ken Dryden and journalist Roy MacGregor dub hockey "Canada's national theatre."

> On its frozen stage, each night the stuff of life is played out: ambition, hope, pride and fear, love and friendship, the fight for honour for city, team, each other, themselves ... It is a place where the monumental themes of Canadian life are played out—English and French, East and West, Canada and the U.S., Canada and the world, the timeless tensions of commerce and culture, our struggle to survive and civilize winter.

And in the *New Brunswick Telegraph Journal*, respected author David Adams Richards plumbs the depths of his thesaurus in trying to capture the elusive truth behind hockey.

> Hockey has always been Canada's ballet, its passion, its main obsession, its spiritual identity, and even its cause for unity ... It is an irreverent flaunting of exhilarated strength, passion and dexterity brought with precision into focus, to create great poetry in front of our eyes.

Or consider the full flightof symbol- laden fancy taken by Bruce Kidd and John MacFarlane in *The Death of Hockey*.

> Hockey is the Canadian metaphor, the rink a symbol of this country's vast stretches of water and wilderness, its extremes of climate, the player a symbol of our national struggle to civilize such a land ... In a land so inescapably and inhospitably cold, hockey is a dance of life, an affirmation that despite the deathly chill of winter we are alive.

By now we are sailing through the stratosphere: hockey as soul, as theater, as venue where monumental themes are played out—hockey as the very dance of life. Perhaps it's time we took it back down to earth, and who better to do that than an American. Here is what sports columnist Jimmy Breslin had to say about the Canadian affinity for hockey (as quoted by Stephen Brook in *Maple Leaf Rag*): "Canadians can't play baseball because baseball is a summer game and Canada has no summer. Canadians should stick to their native sports, namely, hockey and pelt trapping."

Ouch. The problem one faces when writing about hockey is coming up with a unique grandiloquent description. I mean, what could one possibly add to all that? I suppose I could call it "The Game of Our Lives," but broadcaster Peter Gzowski beat me to it. Or I could slip deeper into aphorism and say "Hockey is the Canadian specific," but poet Al Purdy said that already.

The best lines having all been taken, I find I have little to add, except this: hockey is not a ballet or a social-economic-political theme, or even a dance of life. It is a damn fine sport. It may inspire metaphors and mythology and epiphanies, and it may help identify that elusive Northern Soul, but above all it is a reckless, wild contest, the fastest contact sport on earth, chess at 300 miles an hour.

Okay, maybe that is going a bit far, but it sure is a fun game.

Canada's Game?

Oddly enough, for all its sentimental, mystical appeal in the Great White North, hockey was not officially declared Canada's national sport until May 12, 1994. And even then, it was named the nation's official *winter* sport. Canada's official summer sport is still, inexplicably, lacrosse.

Blood on the Ice

Besides its speed and adrenaline, hockey—at least as it is played by men—is also known for its testosterone. The wild aspects of the game, hockey as anarchy on a leash, also creates a dark side: the vulgar machismo of hockey violence. Fighting in hockey, the "rock 'em/sock 'em" style, is the visceral equivalent of pornography—but with less value. It's a voyeur's thrill.

Hockey has always been a rough-and-tumble sport. When the first indoor public game was played in Montreal in 1875, several women in the audience walked out in protest at the level of violence. And remember, this was during a game that was supposed to help promote the sport.

Newspapers were demanding an outright ban on hockey as early as 1864, calling the game "annoying and dangerous." The *Ottawa Citizen*, in 1904 already calling for stiffer penalties and a ban on fighting, noted, "The finest game in this world to watch, hockey, as our leading Canadian teams play it, is being made a byword and a disgrace by the manner in which matches are conducted and foul play tolerated."

One early tough guy, appropriately named Sprague Cleghorn, was said to have taken part in at least "50 stretcher-case fights." Once, in 1912, after a vicious fight with a player named Newsy Lalonde, both Sprague and Newsy were arrested and thrown in jail. As historian Mary Malone writes, Sprague's manager "arrived to find them both in the same cell playing a friendly game of craps with the bail bondsman."

Back in Canada's imperially minded days, when the monarchy still commanded respect and deference, arena owners discovered that hockey fights could be ended by playing "God Save the King" over the loudspeakers. As the scratchy record player began the anthem, the players would stop and stand in respectful silence. Sometimes, one rendition was not enough. As hockey historian Garth Vaughan recalls:

Many of us remember a vicious fight that was broken up one night by playing the anthem: the players stood at attention until the last strains of the anthem finished, only then to start fighting again. The anthem began once more, and the players suddenly stood at attention. It had to be played three times before the players finished their fight.

The Gentler Gender?

In 1976, three Philadelphia players were charged with possession of a deadly weapon and assaulting a police officer—during a game, no less. One of the players had been sent to the penalty box, where an obnoxious fan started spitting on him. When the player tried to decapitate the fan with his stick, a police officer intervened. The player's teammates came to his rescue, the stick swinging began, and the crowd fled. (It was this type of bizarre violence that Paul Newman spoofed in the classic hockey satire *Slap Shot*.)

The violence that was such a trademark of the Philadelphia Flyers during the 1970s earned the team the nickname "Broad Street Bullies." It also turned off an entire generation of women.

Mind you, women aren't entirely immune from the allure of violence. In 1988, Trudy Banwell became the first female hockey player ever to be convicted of assault, when she went after both the linesman and the referee. Charged with two counts of assault (she had separated the linesman's shoulder during the fight), Trudy was given a conditional discharge and banned from hockey for life.

Fighting has always been a part of hockey and probably always will be. Although hockey violence can—and should—be controlled better than it has been, attempts to banish fighting outright have inevitably failed. The amount of padding players wear makes the body blows look worse than they are. Hockey, after all, is a high-adrenaline, hard-hitting game.

And if you disagree with me, I'll drop my gloves and deck you.

What the Heck is Going ON?
Rules and Basic Positions

Okay, girls, here's the truth: hockey is an easy game to follow, with simple rules. The "hockey guy" likes the game to seem complicated, because this allows him to speak to you in long, boring, convoluted sentences peppered with technical jargon and mind-numbing statistics. He thinks this makes him seem smart. Whatever.

When I first started watching hockey, I didn't know what was going on. It seemed like the announcers were speaking in tongues; they were using names I didn't know, and terms that made no sense at all. The referees were constantly blowing their whistles, and I always missed the play or the reason for the penalty. The only thing I did catch were the fights. Watching hockey was like learning a different language, and it was very frustrating, at first. But after a few games, I finally had my first Hockey Moment. I was watching the game when suddenly I saw the play, I saw the patterns in what seemed like chaos, the strategy of the players. It happened in an instant: one moment I was normal, the next moment I was a Fan.

This chapter will explain the game and its rules. We will start with the very basics and by the end of this chapter you will understand what the heck is going on.

The Game

A hockey game is sixty minutes long, that is, sixty minutes on the official clock. In real time, it could last anywhere from three hours to what seems like three years.

Overtime

If a regular-season NHL game is tied, the two teams will play five-minute "sudden-death" overtime. The first team to score in that time wins. It's kind of like a bar at closing time: you know you only have a few minutes before the lights go up and if you don't score before then, you will be going home alone. If the players don't score before the five minutes are up, the game is entered into the record book as a tie.

During the playoffs, if the game is tied, the sudden-death overtime has no time limit (it's played in twenty-minute periods).

Be happy you weren't a hockey girlfriend on March 24, 1936. This is the day of the longest overtime ever, during the playoffs between the Montreal Maroons and the Detroit Red Wings. The game went for 116 minutes of overtime, which equals six overtime periods. Modere "Mud" Bruneteau of Detroit finally put the game out of its misery when he scored after nearly three hours of play.

In international and Olympic games, ties are settled by a five-minute sudden-death overtime, and if that doesn't work they have a shootout. Each team picks five players to take a penalty shot at the opposing goalie. The chosen shooters take turns skating in from center ice, by themselves, and taking a shot at the goalie. The team with the most goals at the end of the shootout wins, and if they are *still* tied there is another shootout. It is a highly civilized and incredibly unfair way to settle a game, reducing the sport to a Midway shooting gallery.

Periods

The game is divided into three periods, each lasting twenty minutes. At the start of each period, the teams switch ends, so don't be confused when you see them shooting the opposite way. There is an intermission between periods. It is during these intermissions that we are entertained by such hockey yammerers as Don Cherry or the wonderfully sweaty players.

Helpful Hint: Pretend the hot and sweaty hockey player is talking about sex instead of the game. This little trick is highly amusing and helps pass the boring intermission. player: we are goin' at it pretty hard out there. I don't know if we can keep it up. But we've been goin' down deep in the zone and I think we'll score soon.

" Pssst... "

The Rink

North American rinks are 200 feet long and 85 feet wide. The boards around the ice are 3½ to 4 feet high and are topped with shatterproof glass, protecting the spectators and keeping the puck in play. It's like a giant playpen.

The Ice Surface

At first glance, the ice surface looks like an alien landing pad, but it is really quite simple. There are lines, circles, and spots. These markings are made after the ice is formed, either with ribbons (Oh, how pretty) or paint. The markings are then covered with several thin, protective layers of ice. Simply, they consist of:

blue lines   **red lines**

goal line

face-off circles

neutral zone

Lines

There are five lines on the ice surface. These lines extend all the way across the width of the ice surface and up the side of the boards.

The red center line divides the ice in half.

There are two blue lines, each 30 feet from the red center line. These blue lines define zones. The center ice between the two blue lines is the "neutral zone." From the blue line to the end of the rink is the team's zone ("offensive" or "defensive," depending on which side you're on).

At each end of the rink, 11 feet from the boards, are the red goal lines. The goal lines are where the goalie's net sits. The goal net is 4 feet high and 6 feet wide. The nets used to be fastened to the ice with immovable pins, but the problem with this was if a player hit it (thunk), there was no give. The metal pins were then replaced with magnetic pins and posts. The problem now was that, if a player even bumped the net, it became unhooked and the play had to be stopped. These days nets are fixed with stiff rubber pins that hold during regular play but will give if they are hit hard. In front of the goalie's net is a blue semicircle; this is the goalie's "crease."

Circles

There are five red, 15-foot, face-off circles painted on the ice. The circle on the red center-ice line is only for face-offs at the beginning of the period or after a goal. The other circles are for face-offs after stoppages of play. Whenever the play stops, there will be a face-off in the nearest circle. During a face-off only two players, and the referee, are allowed inside the circle.

The face-off was invented by referee Fred Waghorne in the early 1900s. Fred had been refereeing a particularly nasty game in Paris, Ontario. In those days the referee simply dropped the puck between the two center men, yelled "Play!", and got the hell out of the way. Finally, bruised and bleeding, Fred had had enough. He told the players to hold their sticks 18 inches apart; he then stood back a cautious distance and threw the puck between them. The modern face-off was born, and referees were now a bit safer. (Waghorne also introduced the whistle, which replaced the hand-held bells refs had been using until then.)

Spots

There are four red spots painted in the neutral zone (between the blue lines). These spots are for face-offs in that zone.

So now you understand the ice: it's just lines, circles, and spots—kind of like your face before you put on moisturizer and makeup.

Player Positions

A team consists of a coach, his or her assistants, a manager, his or her assistants, several trainers, equipment managers, team doctors, and about twenty players. The team usually has twelve forwards, six defensemen, and two goalies, and carries extra players in case there are injuries during a game. These players must sit on the bench, waiting to be called, and remain focused on the game.

During a hockey game, there are six players on the ice at a time: the goaltender, two defensemen (left and right), and three forwards (left wing, center, and right wing).

Most teams rotate three or four forward lines. The forward's job is to get the puck in the offensive zone and set up the goal, and the center forward tries to win face-offs. Forwards are fast skaters and hard shooters. They are the best at frequent, lustful quickies.

The defensive line is rotated two or three times, and their job is to stop the attacking team at all costs. These guys are the hard checkers. Sticks, boards, or body parts: they'll use anything to get in the way. Defensemen are best at long, hard romps in the sack.

The goaltender usually plays the whole game; the back-up goalie comes in as a replacement only if the starting goalie is hurt or not playing well. Goalies are the real mad men of the league, guys who choose to throw themselves in front of an object going up to 90 miles per hour, sacrificing whatever body part is needed. Goalies are the crazed lovers who will do anything—anywhere—anytime.

Players generally stay on the ice for shifts lasting between forty-five seconds and two minutes. Remember, these guys skate in short bursts at speeds up to 30 miles an hour. The line changes happen "on the fly," which means they rotate the player's lines while the game is being played. Hockey is the only sport that does this. Changing "on the fly" is a very tricky maneuver, because if there is any confusion and not enough players are on the ice, the team is vulnerable; too many players on the ice will cost them a two-minute minor penalty. To try to prevent confusion and weakness, the players switch when they have taken the puck to the red line and dumped it into the offensive zone, or between stoppages of play.

The Equipment

The Puck

The puck is a 5 ½- to 6-ounce blob of rubber mixed with coal dust. The rubber has been cooked under pressure (vulcanized), formed into a sausage shape, and sliced like a jelly roll. It is 1 inch thick and 3 inches wide, and is frozen. (A frozen puck slides better and bounces less than a warm one.) It is the home team's responsibility to supply the rubber for a game.

Skates

Nothing is more important to a hockey player than his skates (okay, one thing is more important, but it isn't needed for the game). Basic skate design has not changed much in thirty years, but the materials they are made of has. Skate boots used to be made entirely of leather, now they are made of Clarino (a synthetic leather), ballistic nylon, Kevlar, and graphite. The heel and lace eyelets are still made of leather. The runners are made of plastic into which metal blades are fitted. The skate blades vary slightly in shape, depending on the player's personal choice and playing position.

Goalies' skates have a slightly different design but are made of the same materials. The boots of goalies' skates have a protective plastic shell to deflect the barrage of pucks slapshot at their feet.

Sticks

Hockey sticks have a shaft and a curved blade, and they are designed for either a right- or left-handed shot. The length of the shaft can be up to 63 inches (Oh, my goodness), and the degree of curve on the blade up to a $\frac{1}{2}$ inch.

Sticks used to be made entirely out of wood. Some modern sticks have shafts made of aluminum, graphite, Kevlar, or titanium, with attachable wooden blades. About half of NHL players use the new sticks, while the other half prefers the feel of wood. The advantage to the newer sticks is that they are lighter, more durable, and cost-effective: if you break a blade, you just replace it instead of the whole stick.

I have always wondered why players tape their sticks, and why, if the stick tape is so important, manufacturers don't put it on right from the start. Well, apparently the stick is taped to the player's personal taste, and a pretaped stick would be an object of scorn and ridicule. The reason for taping the stick is to add grip to the butt end, with either a knob shape or a complex spiral, and the tape on the blade cushions hard passes and provides a clearer target for teammates to pass to. Taping the stick is a ritual, a right of passage for all players, from peewee to pro. A "hockey guy" cannot resist an untaped stick. I once won a Vancouver Canucks teddy bear, and the first thing Bruce did was tape its stick.

Goalies' sticks are shaped differently. They have a wide "paddle" partway down the shaft of the stick to help block shots. Their sticks are made completely of wood wrapped in fiberglass.

Sweaters

When hockey was a game played on frozen ponds and lakes, the players' sweaters were made of wool. Now that we have heated rinks, players wear a much lighter fabric. A hockey team actually has several different sweater styles, one for home games (a lighter-colored jersey), one for away games (a darker-colored jersey), and practice jerseys. The colors of their party jerseys are left to their discretion.

Helmets

Hockey players didn't start wearing helmets regularly until the early 1970s. Now, you would think this revelation would have happened earlier in hockey's history. I know that if I was one of the early players and someone explained that I would be skating on ice with frozen chunks of rubber flying around, the first thing I would have done is grab a bucket and jam it on my head.

Before the 1970s, the only players to wear helmets were people with head injuries (this should have been a clue). The league ruled in the 1979–80 season that anyone coming into the NHL from that moment on had to wear a helmet. The last player on the ice to not wear a helmet was Craig MacTavish, who retired after the 1996–97 season.

Goalies now wear helmets, masks, and neck protectors, but they didn't always. Jacques Plante (see Chapter 9 for more) was the first NHL goalie to wear a mask, in 1959. The last goalie to *not* wear a mask on ice was Andy Brown, in 1973.

Shoulder Pads and Chest Protectors

A basic shoulder pad gives protection to the shoulders, collarbone, and upper arms. Some shoulder pads (those unrelated to 1980s power dressing) extend to give protection to the chest, and down the rear to protect the back and spine. Defensemen usually wear the full shoulder pad for protection against hard checking and for blocking shots. A forward may wear lighter shoulder pads, depending on his style of play.

Goalies, naturally, wear very strong chest pads and are padded down both their arms to their wrists.

Elbow Pads

Elbow pads protect the elbow (duh!) and the sides of the elbow. You do not want a frozen puck hitting your funny bone at 90 miles per hour.

Gloves

Gloves offer protection for the back of the hand, especially the thumb, which is often hit by other players' sticks. The palm of the glove is soft and flexible so the player has a good "feel" for his stick. The cuff extends over the wrist and up the forearm to give protection against sticks, and ice burn from falling on the ice.

The goalies' gloves are quite different. The goalie has a "blocker," a rectangular pad used for blocking shots, on the stick hand. The other glove, the "catcher," looks like a large mitten and is used to catch (what else?) the puck.

Hip, Thigh, Kidney, and Tail-Bone Pads

Most hockey pants are made with built-in padding. If the pants are not padded or the player is looking for more protection, then a padded girdle is an option. That's right, a "padded" girdle.

Leg Guards

Long ago, players used to stuff their pants with old magazines and catalogs. (Hey, are you glad to see me or is that the *Sears Wishbook* in your pants?) These days players have guards to protect their shins and knees, and ones that wrap around to protect their calves.

Goalies have large, pillow-like pads that wrap around the top of their skates and extend up past their knees.

The Cup

Hockey players usually wear a heavily padded boxer-style cup. The players find this style is more comfortable than the smaller, all-plastic ones. To date, no player has opted for the "peek-a-boo" style cup, but I still have hope for next year's draft.

Now that you know these guys are packing a lot of gear under those uniforms, don't be fooled by a cute butt that is attached to a well-padded girdle.

The Rules

For the purpose of clarity (and fun) I will be using two completely fictional NHL teams as examples in the explanation of the rules. The teams will be the Bad Boys (who always break the rules but are handsome devils), and the Beef Cakes (who are *très* buff and never break the rules).

The two important technical rules of hockey are *offside* and *icing*.

Offside

Offside is called when you feel his cold feet crawling onto your warm side of the bed.

Otherwise, there are two ways to get a real offside call.

The first way is called "the two-line pass." The rule is this: when a player passes the puck across two lines (a blue line and the red) to a teammate, it is offside. The referee will blow his whistle, signaling the play dead, and will order a face-off near the point where the offside pass began.

This rule prevents the players from just whacking the puck up and down the ice to each other. This would make the game too sloppy and also make scoring too easy.

Let's look at an example:

Bad Boy No. 21 (a defenseman) is near his own net. He passes to Bad Boy No. 34 (a forward), who is hanging around the far side of the red line, waiting for a pass. Bad Boy No. 34 shoots, scores, and he doesn't even have to move or show any skillful skating. It's too easy.

Another way for an offside call is "the blue-line rule." The play is offside if the attacking player crosses the blue line into the attacking zone ahead of the puck. He can't receive a pass if he has already crossed the blue line, and he can't already be in the attacking zone if his teammate is carrying the puck in. The referee will blow his whistle, signaling the play dead, and will order a face-off in the neutral zone closest to where the puck was received.

This rule prevents a player from skating into the attacking zone and waiting for a pass. Again, it would make scoring far too easy.

Here come our boys to illustrate the blue-line rule:

Bad Boy forward No. 11 is at center ice (the red line). He sees Bad Boy forward No. 88 crossing the blue line into the Beef Cakes' zone. Bad Boy No. 11 thinks the referee is a dumb goof, so he passes the puck to Bad Boy No. 88 (who is waaay past the blue line). Bad Boy No. 88 receives the pass, and it is whistled offside by the not-so-dumb-and-goofy referee.

Bad Boy No. 46 sneaks over the blue line into the Beef Cakes' zone. He hangs around the Beef Cakes' goal net, trying to look innocent (but he can't because he is so bad). Bad Boy No. 73 gets the puck and carries it into the Beef Cakes' end and passes it to Bad Boy No. 46, who has been hanging around the net, eating a donut, waiting for an easy goal. The play is called and Bad Donut Boy is offside.

The important
thing to remember about offside is that it is the player's skates, not his stick, that determines the offside. This is why our good boys, the Beef Cakes, always straddle the blue line, but are never offside.

Icing

Icing in fantasy is what I want to lick off Mark Messier's bare chest.

Icing in reality is called when a player, positioned on his own half of the ice, shoots the puck down the ice and over his opponents' goal line. Play is stopped when an opponent, other than the goalie, touches the puck. The referee will blow his whistle and order a face-off back where the icing shot came from.

If we didn't have this rule, every time there was a good shot on goal, or the possibility of one, the defending team could just dump the puck into the other end of the rink. This would make the game boring.

Let's call on the boys to give us
a demonstration:

The pressure is on. The Beef Cakes have been slamming the puck at the Bad Boys' goalie. The Bad Boys' defenseman gets the puck and shoots it all the way down the ice, past the Beef Cakes' goal line. The Beef Cakes' defense-man (rumored to have a great ungirdled butt) falls back into his zone and touches the puck. The referee calls it and there is a face-off in the Bad Boys' zone. This puts the pressure and the puck right back in front of the Bad Boys' net. Icing is a bad idea.

There is an exception to the icing rule. A team that is a man short (has a bad boy in the penalty box) may ice the puck as much as they like. This is the only exception to the rule. The icing rule came along because of two games, played between the New York Americans and the Boston Bruins.

On December 8, 1931, the Americans were facing the superior Bruins. To try to keep the puck away from Boston, the Americans would drill the puck out of their zone. They iced the puck a frustrating and boring sixty-one times during that game. After the game, the Bruins' owner, Charles Adams, was royally ticked off. In the next game against the Americans, on January 3, 1932, Boston retaliated by icing the puck eighty-seven times during that game. These were probably the most boring games in hockey history! Shortly after that the NHL president, Frank Calder, announced the icing rule.

Scoring

Although you wouldn't know it at times, the whole point of a hockey game is to score goals. A goal is counted when a puck *completely* crosses the goal line behind the goalie.

There are several reasons for a goal to be disallowed:

- The puck deflected off an official.
- The puck was directed into the net by a high stick (i.e., a stick above the player's shoulder).
- The puck was kicked or batted by a player's glove into the net.
- An offensive player was in the goalie's crease when the goal was scored (interfering with the goalie).
- The goalie was in the crease, buck naked, covering himself in whipping cream and dirty-dancing with his goal posts.

In some cases the referee may not be able to see what happened with a goal, and so he will consult the goal judge or the video goal judge. The goal judge sits behind the goalie (off ice) and is responsible for turning on the red goal light when the puck crosses the goal line. From this vantage point the goal judge can see the plays well, but even if he thinks the goal he witnessed will be disallowed he must turn on the goal light to signal the puck crossing the line. The video goal judge has a video replay to review questionable goals and, if the referee feels it is warranted, he will call the video judge to clarify. Ultimately the referee has the final word on allowable goals. The referee is the Goal God.

The player who puts the puck in the net is credited with the goal; the player (or players) who passed the puck to the scorer is credited with an assist. No more than two assists are given per goal. A player who gets either a goal or an assist gets a point on his record and it is added to his personal statistics.

A Few Tips on Watching a Game

If you keep your eyes on the puck, you are going to catch most of the plays. If you do miss a big play, then TV coverage, and some arenas, have those helpful instant replays.

A little tip I learned: if you don't understand why the ref blew his whistle and there didn't appear to be a penalty, the ref is probably calling offside or icing.

In the beginning, don't worry if you can't understand the play-by-play announcers; you'll get used to their babble (and actually appreciate it when you need a potty break). Once you are more comfortable with the game, you can let your eyes wander to your favorite player to see how he's doing or who the opposition's coach put on to guard him. Don't forget to listen for the puck sounds (off the glass or the goal posts), the players' naughty banter, and, my favorite, the crunching and moaning of the unlucky players on the boards.

Appropriate Insults

Now that you've got a few tips on how to watch the game, it's time to learn the appropriate insults to use for the ref and the players. You don't want a room full of bellowing hockey fans to fall silent in disgust when you call a nasty player a "goof" instead of the appropriate term, "goon." Here are a few case scenarios and suitable utterances.

A player is playing well and taking many good shots on goal but he just can't get it by the goalie.
Response: "He's been snake-bitten!" "He's jinxed!" "He was robbed!" Or, my all-time favorite, "That goalie's got a horseshoe up his ass!"

A player is waiting around the center line, looking for easy shots and cheap goals.
Response: "What a cherrypicker!"

A player winds up for a big dramatic swing and shot on goal that doesn't do much damage (and looks really stupid).
Response: "Nice golf shot!"

A player is trying to draw a penalty and pretends to be tripped, making a thespian attempt at falling.
Response: "Nice dive. Maybe you'll get an oscar for that one!" Or

"Way to go, claude" (i.e., claude Lemieux, who takes more dives than an olympic Platform team).

A player has been hit from behind.
Response: "He was cold-cocked!" or (if he is on the opposing team) "Good clean hit!"

A player has an opposing player on the boards. He gives him a low elbow, then again, raising his elbow to mid-shoulder, and finishing with a third blow at shoulder height. Gordie Howe was famous for this 1-2-3 elbowing maneuver, and was sometimes called "Mr. Elbow."
Response: "Who does he think he is? Gordie Howe?" or "Hey, that was a Howe elbow!"

A team is playing a rough game, relying on their size, strength, and dirty techniques.
Response: "What a bunch of goons!" "Goon squad!" or "Bunch of ice thugs!" or, if they are your team, "Good hard-hitting hockey!"

A player has been sent to the penalty box.
Response: "He's off to the sin bin!" If it's your team, "What a rip-off! He didn't do nothin'! That guy's teeth fell out on their own!"

A team is ending the regular season with no hope of making it to the playoffs.
Response: "Looks like they're ready for the golf course."

A player has had a long career, his game is not what it used to be, and there are rumors of his retirement.
Response: "Looks like it's time to hang up the blades."
(Warning: This is a powerful phrase which could weaken any hockey guy like kryptonite could Superman. Never, never use it in reference to your guy's favorite player.)

Now that you understand the player positions (non-sexual), the basic rules (frozen tootsies and licking Marky), and a few tips on watching the game (including appropriate insults) you are suited up and on your way to being a hockey fan.

Why are they Always Blowing the Whistle?

Penalties and Signals

I Went to a Fight and a Hockey Game Broke Out ...

If watching a hockey game is a new experience for you, you may wonder why they don't just start the game with *everyone* in the penalty box. Then they could just let out those who *did not* display a maniacal, blood-lust-driven need to decapitate their fellow players. It would be kind of like being paroled from prison, given time off for good behavior, that kind of thing. Also, if you are unfamiliar with the game, you may be led to believe that every single player on the ice has done something very personally wrong to every other player on the ice. They seem very, very mad.

The truth is, hockey is a physical game by nature. Unlike baseball, where teams play offense when they are at bat and defense when they are on the field, players in hockey must be prepared to change strategy in an instant. Turnovers are the order of the day; possession of the puck is the key. Since few players will respond to a politely worded request to relinquish control of the puck, it must be taken from them forcibly. Rules and penalties exist to differentiate between acceptable and unacceptable ways of pummeling an opponent into submission.

Minor, Major, and Misconduct: The Penalty Threesome

Penalties come in three different types, depending on the severity of the infraction. The referee decides which punishment fits the crime and he will not be swayed once he makes a decision. Referees are like the parents of the hockey game: "Go to your room and just think about what you've done! Don't argue with me! ... Because I said so, that's why!" The players are the kids: "Yeah but, he started it! I didn't do nothin'!"

Coaches and players will plead their case to the ref whenever they get a chance. The hope is that, if they complain often enough, eventually someone will believe them.

A penalized player must sit in the penalty box for the duration of the penalty. Minor penalties, however, are over if the other team scores. Then it's time for that long, sheepish skate back to the bench. *Jeez. Sorry, coach.*

If a goalie is assessed a penalty, one of the players from his team—who was on the ice at the time of the call—must serve it for him. It's like when the boss's kid screws up; somebody is going to have to pay for it and you know it won't be Junior.

A Minor Indiscretion (The Two-Minute Minor)

A minor penalty is assessed for common infractions such as *holding*, *tripping*, or *hooking*. A particularly savage *slash* or *high stick* will draw a double minor: four minutes in the box rather than two.

A team serving a minor penalty will have four skaters on the ice, versus the other team's five. Two penalized players off at the same time means three defenders against five. Three is the minimum number of players (not including the goalie) that a team will have on the ice, regardless of how many penalties are being served.

If a penalty is assessed to two players from opposing teams at the same time, they serve their time in the box, and each team still plays five skaters a side. These penalties are referred to as *coincidental minors*.

It is possible to get a minor penalty even if you're not on the ice! A *bench minor* may be given for delaying the game with an excessively slow line change or inappropriate comments directed at the officials. As a general rule of thumb, comments concerning a ref's mom, wife, or personal hygiene will usually merit a bench minor.

A Major *Faux Pas*

A major penalty earns a player five minutes of solitude in the penalty

"tripping"
"hooking"
"holding"

box. Major penalties differ from minor ones in that the player must serve the full five minutes even if his team surrenders a goal (or two, or more).

The referee will assess a major penalty for fighting or for more brutal interpretations of lesser penalties. A major penalty given for injuring another player in the face or head will result in a $100 fine from the NHL, which is about 0.001 percent of a player's salary. If a player collects three majors in a single game, he is automatically ejected.

You're in Big Trouble Now, Mister (Misconduct Penalties)

Misconduct penalties come in three degrees of severity: basic, game, and gross.

A *basic misconduct* penalty is worth ten minutes of quiet reflection in the penalty box. During this time, the team does not have to play with fewer players, just without the penalizee.

A *game misconduct* sends a player to the showers early, a good time to catch up on reading or correspondence.

A *gross misconduct* means a player is through for this game and the next game, and there will be a fine and the possibility of more game suspensions.

Minor (Penalty) Hockey: A Primer

Here is a list of the more common no-nos for which you will see players penalized. Some hurt more than others and some are just plain mean.

Boarding

Checking an opponent into the boards is okay as long as a player doesn't get carried away (or as long as his victim doesn't need to be carried away). A boarding penalty is called for use of excessive force in sending another player into the boards, regardless of how he gets there (i.e., tripping, cross-checking, etc.)

Butt-Ending: *Pardonez-Moi?*

Oh, the imagination just soars, doesn't it? Actually, this refers to jabbing an opposing player with the butt end of your stick. In French it is called *donnez six pouces*, or "to give six inches." I'm not even going to touch that one.

Charging: Will That Be Cash Or … *Aaaaaagh!*

Think of a bull charging at the red cape of a matador. Now imagine that the bull is Eric Lindros and the cape is a red-shirted opponent. Get the picture? Charging is called when one player takes an obvious run at another (usually three clear strides in the target's direction before impact) and/or jumps into the opponent. Charging can result in a major or minor penalty, depending on the damage done.

Checking from Behind

This refers to a potentially dangerous infraction. If a player is checked from behind (i.e., checked without being able to see it coming), there is no opportunity to prepare for the impact. Checking from behind can result in serious head and neck injuries if the unfortunate checkee falls into the boards.

Cross-Checking

This involves knocking another player to the ice or into the boards using the stick held across the chest. The motion is the same as a bench press, only standing up rather than reclining.

You will often see cross-checking called when a defender knocks down an opposing player in front of the net as they vie for position. Not to be confused with "cross-dressing." (For more on hockey he-men and the gear they wear, see Chapter 2.)

Delay of Game: Don't Waste My Time

There are many ways a player can get a delay-of-game call against his team. An excessively slow line change, covering the puck and holding it when no attacking players are threatening, and shooting the puck into the stands on purpose are the more common ways of earning a call. If the goalie shoots the puck out of the rink inside his own blue line, he automatically gets two minutes for delay of the game, even if it was a mistake. The puck must clear the glass cleanly in order to merit a penalty; if it rolls off of the glass or tips on the edge, then no penalty is assessed. Of course, goalies don't have to serve the penalty. Someone else takes it for them.

Elbowing

Civilized individuals use their elbows for leaning and nudging, and occasionally to speed their way through a crowd. Hockey players use their elbows as lethal weapons. Perhaps the most famous elbow *aficionado* was Gordie Howe. When you went into a corner with Howe, you had a choice: watch the elbow and lose the puck; watch the puck, and well, maybe lose consciousness.

Elbowing infractions usually occur when two players go crashing into the boards and raise their arms to protect themselves and/or ding the other guy. More often than not it's the latter.

High-Sticking

Any time a player's stick comes in contact with another player above the shoulders, a high-sticking infraction is called. In the event that blood is drawn, a double-minor penalty will be handed out (four minutes instead of two). An intentional high stick results in a five-minute major and a game misconduct.

Holding: That Loving Embrace

A hockey game is not the place to be if you just want to be held. Not only is holding unromantic during a game, it's worthy of a two-minute penalty.

Holding is a lot like interference, but it refers to actually grabbing someone in order to impede his progress. A holding penalty is also called when a player hangs onto an opponent's stick. Sometimes a player will purposely hold another player's stick between his arm and body to try to make it look like he's being hooked (see below).

Hooking: Two Minutes for Soliciting

When a player uses his stick to impede or haul down another player, the curved blade of the stick is used as a hook to pull on the other player. Hooking in hockey has nothing to do with prostitution or rug-making.

Interference

Interference refers to impeding the progress of another player who does not have the puck (i.e., being a pest). A player can also get an interference penalty if he knocks an opponent's stick out of his hands or prevents him from picking it, or any other piece of equipment, up again (i.e., being a pest).

In the latter stages of the 1998–99 season, the NHL began a crackdown on this type of behavior. Referees were instructed to tighten up on excessive interference in an attempt to speed up the game. While it seems

like calling more penalties would serve to slow the game down, the intent was actually to speed things up.

Kneeing

The NHL takes a very dim view of kneeing infractions—a severe knee injury can be a career-ender—so referees are quick to make the call. The most common instance is when two players are passing each other and one puts his leg out to hit the other knee-on-knee. A flagrant knee (sounds like a species of tropical flower) will result in a double minor or a major for deliberate attempt to injure, along with possible fines and suspensions.

Roughing

Some players like it rough, but it doesn't turn referees on at all. Roughing is called when one player pushes, shoves, strikes, or otherwise abuses another. A roughing call will usually result from an altercation that promises—but never actually delivers—a flat-out fist fight.

Slashing

Using the stick as a scythe: a two-handed swing with a hockey stick can really hurt, especially if it finds a gap in the padding.

Spearing: As Mean as It Sounds

Spearing is the companion penalty to butt-ending. It refers to stabbing at an opponent with the blade of the stick instead of the other end. I don't want to know what the French call it.

Tripping

Not a hard one to figure out. Some players will execute a graceful swan dive when they feel a stick at their feet, in an attempt to draw a tripping penalty. Claude Lemieux was an expert at this.

Too Many Men on the Ice

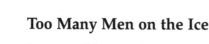

Some would argue that too many men is a contradiction in terms, like too much chocolate. In the NHL, however, a team can have only six players (goalie included) on the ice at any one time. Occasionally, a lack of communication on the bench will result in six or more skaters heading up the ice.

The opposition will always be more than ready to notify the referee if a team has too many men on the ice.

Unsportsmanlike Conduct: You Take That Back!

I'm not exactly sure what "sportsmanlike conduct" is or why it is held in such high esteem. I assume that everything that players do that *doesn't* earn them a penalty is considered sportsmanlike. Now there's a scary thought.

An unsportsmanlike conduct penalty is usually given for overly exuberant discussion of an opponent's or official's genealogy. On-ice talk can get very racy, but there are limits to how much and what kind of abuse referees are willing to put up with.

Fighting: On the Street It Would Be Assault

The world of professional hockey is a strange place indeed. If I were to walk up to someone at work who has been getting on my nerves (you know, hogging the photocopier, burning the coffee) and slug him, they'd haul me into court in a second. In a hockey game, however, all of my friends would cheer and my punishment would be five minutes at a different desk with nobody to bug me.

Fighting in the NHL (officially referred to as "fisticuffs"—sounds rather gentlemanly and distinguished, doesn't it?) is considered by many to be a part of the game. They argue that, if fighting were not an option, the result would be an increase in dirty stickwork. Seems these boys just need an outlet for their frustrations. Hmmm. The answer seems obvious, doesn't it?

A Black Eye, a Bloody Nose, and ...

Fighting will get you a five-minute major and an additional two if the referee deems that you are the instigator. The "third man in," that is, any player who joins in on an existing fracas, will also be spending two minutes in the box.

In recent years, the NHL has tried to curtail fighting by introducing the third-man-in rule and by levying fines against not just the players but the teams themselves. Gone are the days of the bench-clearing brawl. In earlier times, it was not uncommon to see every player from both benches jump over the boards and pair up in battles ranging from the sweater-holding "dancing" variety to the flat-out punch-fest.

> **Bruce:**
> Ah, those were the days.

> **Will:**
> Hear, hear!

Why Don't the Refs Stop Them?

When you see two players squaring off after a heated exchange, you may be wondering why the referee and linesmen don't jump in and put a stop to it right away. But would you jump in between a pair of 200-pound meatheads swinging their fists blindly? Exactly. The officials would rather let them take it out on each other and step in after the players have tired themselves out. Even then, however, it's not always safe to break up a couple of determined scrappers. Somebody is always looking to get that last good shot in before heading off to serve penalty time.

They Like It on Top

The strangest phenomenon associated with fighting is the oddly disconcerting "I'm on top so I win" theory. Time and time again, players will exchange punches until one of them manages to catch the other off-balance and throw him to the ice. For some reason, players and fans alike will respond as if the player who lands on top has won the fight, regardless of the pounding he may have taken while still on his feet. I suspect it stems from some kind of latent primal instinct to establish dominance. There could be a lengthy research project here for a resourceful sociologist. Or maybe Jane Goodall can explain it all.

> **Will:**
> Are you suggesting some kind of correlation between gorillas and hockey players? I'm shocked.

> **Bruce:**
> You're right. That's a slur against gorillas.

Meet My Body Guard

When Wayne Gretzky played for the Oilers, his teammate Dave "Cement Head" Semenko had a very simple job. His job was to keep an eye on Wayne and, if anyone tried to hurt Wayne, then they had to answer to Dave. Dave was very, very big. To Oilers fans, he was an enforcer; to everyone else, he was a goon. Still, players thought twice before they took a run at Gretzky.

Goon or enforcer, Semenko and players like him did and do serve a purpose. Lately, the NHL has become a place where a real talent for the game makes you popular not only as a player but as a target.

Born to Hand Jive, Baby: Additional Hand Signals and Calls

Referees use hand signals for more than just calling penalties. They also have moves to express their motivation for various other stoppages of play. I get the feeling that referees are moments away from breaking into an interpretive dance routine. If only they could lose their inhibitions—and the whistle.

Gloved Ahead

The referee indicates that the puck has been advanced up-ice with a player's hand by making a scooping motion alongside his body. It looks like he's patting the butt of an imaginary friend.

Goal

A goal is signaled by pointing at the net which has just received the puck and blowing the whistle. This signal often goes unnoticed because of the thousands of people yelling and the sirens going off and the fireworks, the spotlights, the laser effects, the shouting of the announcers … Kind of makes you wonder why the refs bother.

No Goal

A disallowed goal is indicated by a double sweeping motion across the waist. A similar signal might be useful to alert a date that his prospects for the evening are nil. The implication in hockey is slightly different

though. It means you didn't score this time, but it makes no predictions about whether you will later.

Match Penalty

A match penalty is signaled by patting the top of your head with one hand (rubbing your tummy with the other is optional). A player being assessed a match penalty is kicked out of the game.

Misconduct

To signal a misconduct penalty the ref places his hands on his hips. It gives him a look of indignation and contempt that says: "Well, I never! You just get over to that penalty box, young man, and no talking back!"

Offside, Delayed Offside, Penalty, Delayed Penalty, Icing

These signals are all essentially the same. The non-whistle hand is held directly over the head as if you have a question for the teacher. In the penalty and delayed-penalty calls, the official points at the offending player. Offsides are signaled by the linesmen.

Penalty Shot

A penalty shot (one player going in, alone, against the goalie) is indicated by the ref crossing his arms over his head with his fists clenched. It kind of looks like your hands are bound above your head. Those kinky little devils.

Penalty shots are usually given when a player who takes an opponent down on a breakaway or covers the puck with his hand in his own crease.

Time Out

"Time out" is a fairly universal signal, making a "T" with one hand held perpendicular to the other. Each team is allowed one thirty-second time-out per game. Time out must be called during a regular stoppage in play. Most teams will save their time-out for the end of the game, or use it to slow things down and regroup if they are in trouble.

4

What's with all the Jargon?
Sports Announcers and the Language They Speak

Probably the biggest obstacle for new viewers trying to understand hockey is the jargon used by the announcers. They seem to be speaking a different language. When a sportscaster says, "Messier, playing short-handed, dekes out the goalie and puts it in the five-hole for a hat trick," you need a decoder ring to figure it out. In this chapter we present a list of the more common (and more confusing) bits of hockeyspeak that you are likely to encounter.

Back on Their Heels

This does not refer to the return to dress shoes after a comfortable vacation spent barefoot on the beach. Instead, it describes a team that finds itself floundering under the pressure being mounted by its opposition. A sudden shift of momentum, whether by a goal or simply heavy pressure in the defensive zone, can leave a team "back on their heels."

Back-Checking

Skating back from the opposition's zone and defending your own zone and goal against an oncoming attack.

Body-Checking

Using your body to hit another player and force him off of the puck. Legal body-checks must be confined to the zone between the knee and the shoulder.

Bad-Checking

Trying to pass a check when you know that you don't have enough money in your account to cover it. You don't want to do this to a hockey player.

Backhand Shot

A shot taken by sweeping the puck backward on the back of your stick, as opposed to forward on the front.

Breakaway

When you find yourself all alone with the puck and no one between you and your opponent's goalie, you are on a breakaway. The breakaway is one of the most exciting plays in hockey. Goalies hate breakaways.

Caught with His Head Down

Being caught with your head down is usually something of which you will have only a vague memory. It happens when you are skating while looking down at the puck or in another direction and fail to see the speeding opponent bearing down upon you. The next sound you hear is often that of an ambulance.

Chippy Play

Chippy play or a chippy player is excessively rough or dirty. Claude Lemieux, Eric Lindros, and Gordie Howe could be called chippy players. The phrase comes from the old saying about having a chip on your shoulder.

Clearing the Zone

Your singular goal while killing a penalty. Shooting the puck out of your zone and down the ice forces the attacking team to fall back and regroup. Clearing the zone is also important during five-on-five play, getting the puck out of your zone and mounting your own attack. It is important to note that, when killing a penalty, shooting the puck the length of the ice doesn't bring an icing call. When you're playing shorthanded, you can shoot at will.

Cut Down the Angle

When a goalie sees a player advancing with the puck, he will often skate out of the net a bit to cut down the angle. There is no complex geometry going on here, it is really quite simple. Imagine the goalie in front of his net with an oncoming player approaching. If the goalie stays in close to his net, the player sees all of the spaces around him where he can shoot the puck. However, if the goalie moves out, he appears bigger by virtue of being nearer the shooter, and therefore covers more of the net. If you don't believe me, try this: Hold a playing card at arm's length and frame it in a doorway across the room. Now move the card toward your face. Ta-dah! The card is cutting down the angle.

Deflect/Redirect/Tip the Shot

This involves changing the path of a shot on goal, usually with the blade of your stick. This confuses the goalie and increases the chance of a goal. Sometimes the puck will deflect off of the body of an unsuspecting player—it still counts as a goal. A puck deflected into the net off of an official doesn't count. Defending players will also try to redirect the puck away from their own net.

Deking or Deking Him Out of His Shorts

To deke (from the word decoy) means to confuse or misdirect an opposing player when carrying the puck. Deking usually involves feigning a move in one direction and going in the other (see also "Head Fake," "Faking the Shot," "Undressing," below). "Deking him out of his shorts" is an extreme case of deking. It suggests that you not only confused your opponent, but could have taken the time to snatch his boxers as well.

Dipsy-Doodle

Not a concession-stand treat on a stick. Rather, a combination of deft stick-handling and skating which allows you to pass by one or more opposing players with the puck. Gretzky is the king of the dipsy-doodle.

Draw a Penalty

To goad another player into taking a penalty without incurring one yourself (see also "Taking a Dive"). Pesky, chatty players like Claude Lemieux are good at drawing other players into taking penalties.

Dropping the Gloves

Throwing your gloves off in order to fight. Kind of like tossing the gauntlet. It is almost chivalrous in a crude, hockey sort of way.

Dump It In

Shooting the puck into the other team's zone without pursuing it. This is usually used to buy time for a line change.

Dump and Chase

A style of play that involves, oddly enough, dumping the puck into the offensive zone and chasing after it. This is an alternative to trying to carry the puck into the zone and maintain possession. It can make for boring hockey.

End-to-End Hockey

An exciting brand of hockey in which both teams alternately launch attacks into the opposition's zone. Usually accompanied by fast skating, sharp passing, and exciting scoring chances.

Enforcer/Goon

Refers to a player who is better known for his physical play than anything else. "Enforcer" doesn't necessarily have the connotation of cheap or dirty play that "goon" does. In the 1970s, Philadelphia Flyers comprised mainly goons.

Fake the Shot

To draw your stick back slightly as if you are about to shoot, and instead pass or continue to carry the puck. Faking the shot can cause the goalie to commit and render him helpless against a subsequent shot. You can also fake a pass to the same effect. Hockey is the only activity where men don't mind if you fake it.

Feather a Pass

Sounds kind of kinky, doesn't it? Sadly, it doesn't mean meeting a swarthy forward standing on the blue line with a feather in his teeth and a come-hither look in his eye. It refers only to a light, gentle pass that lofts over the opposition's stick(s) and alights on that of your teammate. This is one of the few non-violent images in hockey. Savor it.

Forcing the Goalie to Commit

Sadly, this is not a sure-fire strategy to force a proposal from your favorite netminder. As far as I know, goalies are no more likely to commit to a relationship than anyone else.

It really means to deke the goalie out so that he commits to blocking the shot that he thinks is coming. This leaves him out of position, and thus vulnerable.

Fore-Checking

Putting pressure on the other team when they have possession of the puck in their own zone. Fore-checking enables you to keep the puck in the opposition's zone and away from yours.

Freezing the Puck

Stopping the play by jamming the puck up against the boards with your skates, stick, or both. The puck must be frozen as a result of fending off an opposing player (or two). You can't just do it for fun or you get a two-minute minor for delay of game.

From the Slot

The slot is that valuable piece of real estate that lies directly in front of the goalie. Taking a shot from the slot gives a better chance of scoring, especially if you have a teammate in front of the goalie (see also "Setting Up the Screen," "Having a Man in the Slot").

Getting Good Wood on It

Making good contact with the puck, resulting in a powerful shot. Not getting good wood on your shot or, worse, missing it altogether, is called "fanning on the shot" and is considered a humiliating lack of finesse.

Give and Go

Passing the puck to a teammate only to receive it back after safely eluding defensive players. Very tricky. Very cool.

Gloved Ahead

A no-no, this occurs when the puck is thrown or moved ahead (that is, in the direction of the opposing goal). A gloved-ahead pass is whistled dead, and a face-off ensues.

Go Down to Block a Shot

Blocking shots requires skill and dedication, either that or a total lack of concern for your personal well-being. As you can guess, it requires you to dive in front of an oncoming shot to prevent a scoring chance. I thought that only Secret Service guys guarding the president were asked to do things like that. With the puck traveling at upwards of 90 miles per hour, you had better hope that you get your shin pads and not your head in its path.

Handcuffed

Not as kinky as it sounds. When the puck is shot high to the chest area of the goalie, he is often said to be handcuffed by the shot (i.e., he has trouble handling it).

Hat Trick (Natural Hat Trick)

A hat trick is the impressive feat of scoring three goals in the same game. The term comes from the English game of cricket. Three wickets and your teammates would buy you a new bowler hat. Spiffy, what? In more recent times, a hockey hat trick would be celebrated with a shower

---

of hats from the crowd. Unfortunately, whereas in the old days a player might pick up a nice fedora and a toque or two, today it's mostly cheap baseball caps. If a player scores a hat trick on a night that his team is holding a promotional hat giveaway, hoo boy, the hats will fly.

A natural hat trick occurs when the three goals are scored consecutively.

Have a Man in the Slot

Okay, stop that right now. This refers to having a teammate in the highly protected slot area who is able to accept a pass and take/tip a shot on goal or screen the goalie.

Head-Fake

A quick head movement in one direction designed to fool your opponent into thinking that you are going to go that way. When he changes course to follow you, you go the other way. Also useful when you find yourself walking down the sidewalk approaching someone you want to avoid— for example, former bosses, in-laws, old boyfriends, ex-girlfriends of your present boyfriend, or people to whom you lost a hockey bet.

Head-Manning the Puck

When you are breaking out of your own zone, head-manning the puck means passing ahead to the player who is farthest up the ice, leading the attack.

Making a Wholesale Change

Changing most of your players on the ice for fresh players. (Strange that a player on ice is considered less fresh than one sitting on the bench …) A wholesale change on one side usually results in one on the other side as well. This allows coaches to match their lines up (see "Matching Lines").

Matching Lines

Coaches know who they want to put on the ice to defend against opposing players. They match lines. For example, you wouldn't ask 5'6" 180-

pound Theo Fleury to cover 6'4" 230-pound Eric Lindros, unless you had a grudge against Fleury.

One-Timer

Although it sounds similar, this is not the same as a one-night stand. It refers to taking a shot as soon as the puck comes to you rather than waiting around to see if a more promising play develops. Hmmm ... okay, so it is kind of the same. In this case, however, you don't have to feel uncomfortable when you next meet the puck.

Open It Up

When one or both teams start to play more offensively-minded, they are said to "open it up." This usually results in more shots and scoring chances as the defensemen move up into the offensive zone to take part in the play.

Penalty Shot

A penalty shot is like an official, organized breakaway. If a player is hooked, tripped, or interfered with while on a breakaway, the referee may call a penalty shot.

The puck is placed at center ice and all players, except the player who has been awarded the shot, and the opposing goalie, are required to leave the ice. When the referee blows the whistle, the player collects the puck and skates in on the goalie. Only one shot is allowed; you can't score on a rebound, and you can't stop along the way.

A penalty shot is also awarded if a player covers the puck with his hand in his own goal crease in order to prevent a goal. Only the goalie is allowed to cover the puck with his hand.

Playing Shorthanded

This refers to playing while one of your teammates is serving a penalty. Your team has one fewer player, therefore, you are shorthanded.

Play Is Whistled Dead

Not as sad as it sounds. Whenever the whistle is blown, the puck is deemed dead. This means that any further movement by the puck is inconsequential. This can be extremely frustrating (or extremely welcome, depending on whose side you're on) when the puck crosses the goal line just after the whistle blows.

Playing the Trap (Neutral-Zone Trap)

A defensive strategy used to prevent opponents from passing through the neutral zone. Sounds like the point of the game, doesn't it? Actually, it is only one of many strategies available to a coach, and you have to do it right for it to be successful. If you have all of your players up in the neutral zone, a speedy opponent can blow by your defense and streak toward the goal unmolested.

Some fans find that excessive use of the trap makes for dull hockey. The New Jersey Devils are notoriously successful at playing the trap.

Point Man

The point man is the player who is up close to the blue line when his team is attacking. During a power play, players in the corners will pass the puck up to the point man as they vie for position closer to the goal.

Poke-Check

Jabbing forward along the ice with your stick fully extended in order to poke the puck off your opponent's stick. Also used by goalies to prevent a shot from close in.

Pull the Goalie

A team that finds itself down by a goal in the final minute or two of the game will often pull their goalie. The goalie is replaced on the ice by another attacker, and the remaining time is played with six players and no goalie. While it gives you the advantage of an extra player, it also means that you run the risk of having the other team score into your empty net from virtually anywhere on the ice. A select few goalies have even scored empty-net goals (see Chapter 9).

Put It Upstairs

A player scoring into the top corners of the net is said to have "put it upstairs" or "gone upstairs." Asking your hockey guy if he wants to go upstairs after the game is something altogether different. Although scoring *is* usually involved.

Ragging the Puck

Gaining possession of the puck and cruising around the ice surface, usually in an attempt to kill time when shorthanded. Bobby Orr, one of the league's all-time great stick-handlers, once ragged the puck for twenty-one seconds straight against the Atlanta Flames, stopping only when he scored. It was magical.

Ring One Off the Post/Crossbar

Sounds like horseshoes, but it really refers to a shot taken on goal that barely fails to go in and instead bounces off the post or crossbar. The speeding puck bouncing off of the hollow metal post gives a distinct pinging sound that can be heard all around the rink.

Rolls Through the Crease

When the puck passes through the crease without being knocked into the net the announcer will usually say that it "rolls though the crease." Kind of a lazy, non-threatening description of a potential scoring chance.

Scrum

In rugby, a scrum is a brutal primitive ritual—much like a hockey face-off—used to start the play and decide possession of the ball. In hockey, a scrum is the same kind of thing but for no real reason. A scrum usually results when the play has been stopped with a group of players gathered around the puck, some standing, some fallen, some trying to stand up so they can knock someone else down. Generally, making contact with the other team's goalie at the whistle (or just after) will result in an enthusiastic scrum. It kind of resembles a bunch of kids playing "pile on."

Set Up the Box

When killing a penalty, one defensive option is to arrange your four play-ers in a box pattern in the slot. That means two players down low to either side of the goal and two up high. This keeps the attacking players to the outside and less able to set up a good shot. Another option com-monly employed is setting up the diamond. The same configuration of players, but turned forty-five degrees.

Setting Up the Screen (Screening)

Refers to the common practice of positioning yourself in front of the goalie, thus obstructing his view of an incoming shot. Goalies hate this too. Not only can they not see the puck clearly, but the screening player can also redirect the puck at the last second. Screening also carries with it the risk of being plowed by a defending player and/or being dinged by your teammate's shot.

Slap-Shot

A powerful shot accomplished by drawing your stick back to about shoulder height and bringing it down quickly to a point on the ice about an inch behind the puck. The subsequent impact bends the shaft of your stick slightly and the resulting spring-back gives extra boost to the puck as you make contact on the follow-through. A slap shot is difficult to con-trol but looks and sounds impressive. Al McInnis is known for his pow-erful slap shot, as was Bernie "Boom-Boom" Geoffrion.

Sniper

A player known for his deadly accurate shot. A sniper can put the puck exactly where he wants it on goal and as a result is usually a high scorer.

Spinerama

The spinerama is an impressive move employed when defending the puck against an opposing player. Basically, the player with the puck fakes in one direction, let's say right, draws the defender, and then suddenly spins 360 degrees and takes off to the left. This move, when executed correctly, often results in a deke of the "Out of His Shorts" variety.

A spinerama that ends in a sudden shot on goal is very deceptive. Goalies hate that too.

Stick-Handling (Puck-Handling)

Manipulating the puck with your stick in such a way as to protect it from opposing players and maintain possession.

Take a Dive

To fall down as if tripped, hooked, cross-checked, or otherwise interfered with when you really weren't. Taking a dive, when it works, is an effective way to draw a penalty. Referees are often wise to players prone to dive-taking and will ignore their theatrics. Players are sometimes described as having "gone down as if shot" when they're really hamming it up.

Tees It Up

Not the act of creating a bold hairstyle with which to dazzle and distract your opponent. In golf, players tee off at the start of each hole. That is, they set the ball up on a little wooden peg stuck in the ground (tee it up) and take a huge swing at it. This image has been adopted by hockey announcers to describe a similarly powerful slap shot.

Telegraph a Shot

To take a shot so hard and straight that it travels like a telegraph. E-mailing a shot is not a phrase that has caught on as yet, but it seems like a more extreme metaphor to me.

Through the Five-Hole

The possible places to score on a goalie are numbered from one to seven. One to four are, respectively, upper left corner, upper right corner, lower left corner, and lower right corner. Six is under the goalie's right arm, seven under his left. The five-hole and, judging by frequent references by announcers, the most popular hole, is that space between the goalie's legs (the empty space between his pads). Shooting through the five-hole therefore means scoring between the goalie's legs. (Insert your own dirty joke here.)

Ties Him Up

Again, not as kinky as it sounds. When a player gets in the way of another player and hampers his ability to join or continue the play, he has "tied him up."

Traffic

Traffic in a hockey game has the same meaning as traffic on crowded city streets. In hockey, though, the crowd of grimy, honking cars is replaced by a crowd of sweaty, grunting hockey players. The only difference is that you would hate to be stuck in the middle of car traffic.

Traffic in front of the net usually consists of attacking players, trying to screen the goalie (see "Setting Up the Screen") or redirect a shot into the net, jostling for position, with defending players trying to move them along.

Undressed

A companion to being deked out of your shorts, being undressed refers to a play during which you were similarly embarrassed.

Wraparound

The wraparound shot is accomplished by coming out from behind the net with the puck and sweeping the puck into the corner closest to you. Doing so allows you to score while your body is still behind the goal line! Gretzky perfected this move. Goalies hate the wraparound because they have to anticipate which way a player behind them is going to go. Maybe they should have rear-view mirrors.

Wrist Shot

Unlike a slapshot, a wrist shot requires no wind up. That is, you take the shot by sweeping the puck forward instead of drawing your stick back and then making contact. A wrist shot allows for much greater accuracy than a slapshot.

FIVE HOLE

Who's the Boss?

Owners, Coaches, Referees, and Linesmen

Who's Responsible for This Mess?

In this chapter, we discuss the all-important question of who is responsible for professional hockey. Who handles the comings and goings, the training and trashing, the penalizing and merchandising, the promotion and demotion, the glorification and ... ah, forget it. We cover the commissioner, the owners, the coaches, the referees, and the players; who's in charge and who just thinks that he is.

If you're moved to jump right in and start wheeling and dealing in the fast-paced world of pro sports after reading this chapter, we've included a section at the end which tells you how to start a pro team of your very own. A word of warning though: you may want to keep your day job until you see if it all pans out. And it had better be a really, really profitable day job.

From Commissioner to Stick Boy

As in any large organization, the division of power within professional hockey is complex and hierarchical. At the top is the NHL commissioner, who, along with the board of governors, has the ultimate say in league matters. Each NHL team appoints a representative to the board, along with one or more alternates. The board is led by an NHL-appointed chairman.

Marketing, merchandising, and putting players on the Wheaties box is handled by a separate arm of the NHL known as NHL Enterprises, L.P. These are the people responsible for things like, for example, allowing authors to use NHL-registered trademark logos in their book. Kiss, kiss.

Next on the totem pole come the individual team owners and presidents. Owners can be lone individuals or groups or companies.

The field generals of hockey, the coaches and general managers, are often the same person. These individuals rely on a secondary team of helpers and assistants that range from specialized coaches (one for goaltending, for example) and trainers, to equipment managers and stick boys. On ice, of course, the officials are in charge. The referee and two linesmen control the play on the ice, while off-ice officials (video goal judges, goal judges, timekeepers, etc.) provide support.

So, the commissioner is in charge of the league, the owners/presidents are in charge of the teams, the coaches et al. are in charge of the players, and the officials are in charge of the games. But what about the players?

Solidarity Forever: The NHLPA

Players are left in charge of nothing more than their own actions, yet sometimes they still forget (see Chapter 3). The players, like workers for a large company, are unionized and can—and do—go on strike if they feel that they are being treated unfairly. The National Hockey League Players Association (NHLPA) represents and defends the concerns of 640-plus professional players.

You Guys Don't Play Fair, I'm Going Home!

The regular season skated to a halt as the result of a players' strike for the first time in 1992. On April 1 (hmmm ...) the players' association voted unanimously to bring the season to a standstill, a move which threatened to delay the playoffs. There were many bones of contention to be picked that day, including: trading-card revenues (yes, players license their image for use on hockey cards. While I would pay for a likeness of Stevie or Marky, you couldn't pay me to keep some of those mugs in my home), the right to be a free agent, contract length, and what to do with a 1986 pension surplus. (I believe Alan Eagleson handled that one personally.)

The resulting walkout (skateout?) lasted a scant ten days, nothing compared to what loomed in the future. The essential points of the deal amounted to acceptance of a one-year contract and free reign over trading-card earnings for the players. Much to the relief of everyone concerned (not least of which, the fans) play resumed and the playoffs went ahead as planned.

Go Team! ... Uh, Team? Helloooo?

In 1994–95 a players' lockout shortened the NHL regular season to only forty-eight games per team from eighty-two. At the center of the dispute were a proposed rookie salary cap and restrictions on veterans who wanted more freedom to move from team to team. When a deal was finally struck, teams had combined to miss out on a total of 468 games. Players found themselves in January—almost halfway through the season ordinarily—trying to get their "game legs." The New Jersey Devils went on to win the cup that year. Whether or not this counts as a "pure" cup win remains the subject of much debate. A schedule of forty-odd games is more in keeping with hockey in the old days, but back then the season was less than half as long as it is now. (I wonder if that has anything to do with the increase in the divorce rate in recent years?) Also, the number of teams in the league has more than doubled.

No interconference games were scheduled for the shortened season either, so teams that met in the playoffs after the conference finals hadn't played each other yet.

The 1925 Hamilton Tigers: "We won't Play!" The NHL: "Okay."

In 1925, the Tigers of Hamilton, Ontario, had the league's best record and earned a bye in the first round of the playoffs. That is, they were allowed to pass on to the second round without playing a series against another team. Perhaps this time off gave the Tigers a chance to think about the past season in greater detail. That season, the NHL had expanded the playing schedule to thirty games per team from twenty-four.

"Wait a minute," said Hamilton players. "We signed on for twenty-four games! They owe us for those other six!"

Thus enlightened, the team members demanded an extra $200 each as compensation. Team management said no.

"Fine," said the ticked Tigers. "We're not playing any playoff games until you pay up."

NHL president Frank Calder took offense and suspended the whole team. Their season, they were told, was over. Things soon went from bad to worse. The team was sold to a group in New York, renamed the Americans, and the players had to apologize to the NHL and pay fines before they were allowed to join their new team. Players learned an important lesson that day: Striking without representation is very, very stupid.

Where Do They Get These Guys Anyway?

Where do hockey players come from? A question which you are bound to ask yourself when you start following their antics on a regular basis. Just what kind of past experience would lead grown men to act like this?

Hockey players start young. That is, they start playing hockey young. (I don't know what else they start early on.) From tiny tikes who have just learned to skate, to big bad boys who eat, breathe, and sleep hockey, there are more leagues and levels than you can shake a hockey stick at. The young ones get their start in peewee, midget, double-A, triple-A, bantam, et cetera, et cetera. (Just for fun, ask your hockey guy if he was ever a pee-wee.) They eventually move on to high school and college teams, and hopefully on to major junior teams. It is usually from this level that a player will be drafted by a pro team. The draft is held once a year after play has concluded for the season. Eligible players, having been scouted by the NHL teams, gather in a designated city and hope for the best.

Scouting is kind of like courtship. You watch a prospect's moves and see if he has what it takes to go the distance. After weighing the pros and cons carefully, you decide if you want to get involved on a personal level. Sometimes a hot new prospect gets lazy after he has a regular spot in the lineup and you have to send him packing. So next time you find yourself having "the talk" to a fizzling new flame, just tell him that you've decided to send him back to the minors for conditioning.

Back at the draft, team representatives make their selections in turn, one at a time. A drafted player will probably not see any action (that's NHL action) for a while. Most draftees are sent to a minor-league affiliate to get used to the faster pace of the professional game. There are several levels within the minor-league system: the three closest to the top are the East Coast Hockey League (ECHL), the International Hockey League (IHL), and the American Hockey League (AHL). The AHL is the next rung down the ladder from the NHL.

Draft day is the biggest day in a young player's career, the day when he goes from amateur to pro. Sometimes, however, players don't feel quite as honored at their selection as we expect them to. Sometimes they're downright offended.

Lindros and the Nordiques: Thanks for the Sweater, Nanna

It is NHL draft day 1991. Representatives from all twenty-two teams have gathered to pick and choose among the hundreds of young hopefuls who pray for their chance at the big league. Eric Lindros is not praying. He knows as well as anyone that he is the number-one draft choice this year. Also no mystery is the name of the team that has earned first pick in this year's draft. That team is the Quebec Nordiques.

Lindros, all 6'4" and 230 pounds of him, played for the Oshawa Generals (of the major junior Ontario Hockey League) the previous year. He has made it clear that he does not wish to play for the Nords. As the other players anxiously await the sound of their own names crackling over the P.A., Eric sits awaiting the inevitable. He knows he'll be in the NHL this season, and he wants to choose which sweater he'll be wearing when the puck drops. Eric seems pretty cocky. He has a right to be. He is the Canadian Major Junior Player of the Year, having scored a league-leading 149 points.

When the call finally comes, Lindros makes his way forward and up onto the stage, where, as is customary, he is presented with a team jersey and cap. Traditionally, draftees don their new colors and pose for the media. There is much smiling and shaking of hands as the new skater is welcomed into the fold. Not today, however. Young Eric receives his new duds with a mixture of horror and forced good manners familiar to anyone who has ever received one of "those sweaters" from a smiling grandma on Christmas morning.

Yes, Eric did what we all dream of doing. He steadfastly refused to wear the sweater, the cap, or anything else that was presented to him. Furthermore, he refused to go to Quebec and play for the Nordiques.

As the new season approached, Lindros maintained his position. He would *not* play for the Nords and wished to be traded. The Quebec franchise owners said that, if he didn't play for them, then he could stay at home and warm the sofa for all they cared; they would not trade him.

The Nordiques were in a frustrating position. After yet another dismal season, they had the opportunity to acquire the hottest young player to come out of the junior league in years. Lindros was being billed as "The Next One," heir apparent to Wayne Gretzky, "The Great One." Under league rules governing the draft, he was all theirs, a player upon whom to build a Stanley Cup contender. Manna from heaven to a struggling team. There was just one problem: he didn't like them and refused to play with them.

The Nordiques, deciding that resistance was useless, finally bit the bullet and began shopping around for a deal. As a bargaining chip, Lindros was a hot property. Offers were made from teams all around the league, many of whom were willing to deal their seasoned veterans for an up-and-coming talent. Eventually, the Philadelphia Flyers won the right to call him their own. And yes, Eric *would* play for them. In exchange, the Flyers sent goalie Ron Hextall, Mike Ricci, Steve Duchesne, Kerry Huffman, Peter Forsberg, Chris Simon, two future first-round draft picks, and a cool $15 million. The equivalent to a starting line—goalie included—with a spare defensive pair and enough cash to pay the yearly salary of a dozen top players. All this for the rights to a player who had yet to lace them up for his first NHL matchup.

In return, the Flyers got the foundation for a team capable of making a serious run for the cup. Eric centers a forward line affectionately known as the "Legion of Doom."

The Nordiques got sold and moved to Denver. They are now known as the Colorado Avalanche. They won the Stanley Cup in 1996, the year after they relocated. Former Nordiques owner Marcel Aubut is not a well-loved man in Quebec. Go figure.

As Long as You Live under My Roof ... Coach as Father Figure

Players need someone to advise and guide them. Since many young players leave home to play junior hockey while still attending high school, the man they call coach soon becomes a sort of surrogate parent. This strange association carries through right to the big leagues. Grown men though they may be, they are still subject to the rules as laid down by their coach. They can still be grounded (benched), sent to their room ("Hit the showers, pal!") and, if need be, kicked out of the house (traded). Indeed, on more than one occasion players have been subject to punishments that would send the average teenager packing. You think your parents were strict? Read on.

Wild Bill Laforge

In 1984, the Vancouver Canucks were coached (briefly) by Bill Laforge. Having already established his reputation as a raving lunatic by biting the head off of a live lizard just to prove he could, Laforge set about whipping the Canucks into game shape. In training camp, players were divided into squads and played scrimmage games for practice. The losers were forced to run back to the hotel in full gear while the rest bussed it. When that failed to inspire his troops to victory, Laforge organized a special drill. A dozen players were lined up close to the boards, forming a kind of aisle between the boards and themselves. The rest were required to skate down the aisle as their teammates checked them repeatedly into said boards. Hard to see why these guys weren't just brimming with confidence, isn't it? I can only imagine the collective sigh of relief breathed by Vancouver players when GM Harry Neale gave Bill his walking papers after twenty-one games. The Canucks' record under his stellar leadership? Four wins, seventeen losses.

Uh, What's the Rope for, Coach?

Eddie Shore played with the Boston Bruins in the 1930s. As a player, he was a tough talented defenseman. He was a fan favorite and won MVP honors four times. Always an aggressive competitor, Shore barely kept his anger contained and was known to blow his top on occasion. After retiring from the NHL, he became owner of the Bruins' farm team, the Springfield Indians. It was then that his top appears to have blown for good.

Indians' practices were always a unique experience. When Shore felt that his goalie was flopping around on the ice too much, he forced him to practice with a noose around his neck tied to the net. When a winger failed to meet Shore's standards, he was trussed up in a harness attached to the rafters. When his play was deemed to be lacking, whoops!, up he went into the air. What this accomplished I have no idea.

By 1966, the Springfield squad had had enough of Shore's strangeness. They hired a lawyer, one Alan Eagleson, to have Shore removed. It worked. The lawyer, by the way, went on to become executive director of the NHLPA. At the time he seemed like a player's best friend. Unfortunately, where Shore had robbed a few players of their dignity temporarily, Eagleson later robbed the players' association of several million dollars. In 1997, he went to jail. In 1998, he got out again.

Too Many Friends? Become a Referee!

After watching a few hockey games, you may begin to wonder what would possess someone to pursue a career as a referee. The job involves:

- arguing with large angry men (or women) while 15,000-plus other angry people yell at you;
- breaking up fights;
- trying to keep your eye on the puck and all twelve players at the same time;
- skating up and down the ice for upwards of three hours as you dodge flying pucks, sticks, and bodies;
- knowing that, no matter how well you do your job, at least half

of the people in your immediate area will believe that you are not only wrong, but possibly criminally stupid as well.

Sound like fun? These are just the on-the-job activities. When they're not being abused at work, refs spend their time on the road. While NHL teams play half of their season at home, every game is a road game to a referee. Referees aren't allowed to stay in the same hotel as the teams, and fraternization with players and team management is discouraged.

Official Efficiency, Then ...

In hockey's early days, officials weren't always the non-partisan arbitrators that we expect them to be today. Players (both retired and active), league executives, and in some cases fans from the crowd, were often called into service.

Modern-day goal judges should be eternally grateful for their comfy mounted chairs, switch-activated lights, and protective plexiglass. Their counterparts from days gone by, often men picked at random from the hometown crowd, observed the game from a vantage point that was much more, shall we say, immediate. That is, they followed the action while perched on a board on the ice directly behind the net. Defending players often "accidentally" dislodged the goal judge from his post when an opposing scoring chance seemed imminent. If the official survived long enough to signal a goal, he did so by waving a hanky. The ultimate decision as to whether or not a goal counted was left to the goal judge. However, if the referee felt that a mistake had been made, he was empowered to send the offending official back to his seat and call for a new volunteer.

At one time referees were all alone out there, the lone voice of reason, the sheriff with no deputies. A single linesman was added later, but then removed in favor of a second referee. Eventually the league settled on the one referee/two linesmen system that we know today.

In 1998, NHL bosses suggested that perhaps two referees would be a good thing after all. Linesmen got nervous.

... And Now

How do referees get to the NHL today, you ask? In much the same way as players do, in fact. They acquire and hone their skills through on-ice experience. They attend pre-season training sessions to improve their performance and expand their knowledge, just like players do. They work their way up from the minors based on the quality of their performance, just like the players do. They don't, however, earn multimillion-dollar salaries like the players do. Referees are paid by the NHL. There are no bidding wars to land a hot new official, no draft, and no signing bonuses. Not that a referee's salary is anything to sneeze at; pay starts at about $75,000 a year and can reach up to $200,000 annually. Linesmen are well compensated too, starting at $49,000 per year and reaching as high as $110,000. Additional income, up to $29,000 for refs and up to $24,000 for linesmen, is paid to officials who get the nod to enforce the rules during post season play.

So, it would appear that the referees' (and the linesmen's of course; linesmen have feelings too) lot in life amounts to the following: no palling around with co-workers, long road trips, and constant abuse at work. Why, we ask, would anyone opt for this kind of existence? Actually it's very simple. It's the game. They love the game. That's right, referees are *hockey fans.*

For some reason, we are conditioned to believe that those in authority have long since lost any sense of what their job is really about. Think about it. As children, we are convinced that the principal has developed such a deep hatred of children and all things childlike that he remains in the employ of the school system for no other reason but to make our lives a living hell. The boss at work cares only for the bottom line. The politician works for naught but his own greater glory. Police are out-of-control power trippers. And referees are out to destroy the inherent beauty of our favorite sport.

Fact is, it ain't necessarily so, folks. Principals *do* nurture, bosses *do* care, cops *do* serve and protect, and yes, referees *do* love the game. (My omission of politicians wasn't an oversight.)

More often than not, referees are former players who retired from the game for their own reasons but couldn't quite shake the need to be involved. One wonders, though, are referees *really* as impartial as we suppose they must be? Is it possible that a referee (or any other official, for that matter) might just hold one team a little bit closer to his heart than the rest? If so, I suspect the chances are greater that aliens will apply for an NHL franchise than that any official anywhere will admit to favoring one team in particular. Some things are better left unsaid, I guess.

And if the aliens do come, I betcha Don Cherry accuses them of playing like Swedes.

R-E-S-P-E-C-T: Find Out What It Means to a Ref

It is known as the "Have Another Donut, You Fat Pig" incident. The year was 1988. The New Jersey Devils had squeaked into the playoffs for the first time ever and had surprised everyone by making it to the third round, where they faced the Boston Bruins. The teams split the first two games of the five-game series, and then … it happened. Game three was a rout, Boston scored six goals to the Devils' one. Jersey coach Jim Schoenfeld was irate, incensed, infuriated, irked even. Schoenfeld felt that his team had been robbed by referee Don Koharski and he meant to tell him so in no uncertain terms. Laying in wait for Koharski in the hallway after the game, Schoenfeld confronted the ref and his linesmen and blocked their path to the officials' dressing room. Koharski ignored the coach's carrying-on and walked past without a word. Schoenfeld pursued. Hurling insults, he brushed past the officials and tried to play human roadblock again. Once more Koharski and his cohorts remained silent and moved on. Schoenfeld then claimed that the referee had stepped on his foot, and his ranting accelerated to a fever pitch. It is at this point that we may imagine the scene in a Zabruder-esque frame-by-frame slo-mo sequence. Schoenfeld's pressure gauge goes into the red; assistant coach for the Devils, Doug McKay, tries to restrain his raging companion and is pushed away. McKay stumbles and falls into linesman Ray Scapinello. Scapinello collides with the back of a retreating Koharski. Koharski wobbles enough to leave the rubber mat lining the hall and stumbles on the concrete floor. Koharski goes down. As we slow the film down, we can pinpoint the exact moment that Don Koharski loses his cool. Tick, tick, tick, SNAP!

Koharski rises from the floor and, assuming that he has just been assaulted by Schoenfeld, makes a proclamation.

"That's it!" he cries. "You're gone now! You're gone! You're out of here! You won't coach again!"

My, my. And how do we think Mr. Schoenfeld responded? Did he apologize for his outburst and ask Mr. Koharski for forgiveness? Not exactly. As Koharski stormed off to the dressing room, Schoenfeld let rip with those now legendary words:

"You fell and you know it! Go ahead, you fat pig, have another donut!"

How do we know so much about this incident? Through the miracle of videotape, of course. The whole sordid tale was captured by the press and replayed frequently in the days to follow. Koharski was understandably upset by the whole thing and contacted the NHL to register a com-

plaint against Schoenfeld. Unable to locate league president John Ziegler, executive vice-president Brian O'Neill took matters into his own hands and issued a one-game suspension to Schoenfeld. New Jersey's legal types pointed out to a judge that O'Neill had no authority to do so, and a restraining order was issued. Schoenfeld would be allowed to coach game four after all. This did not set well with the officials of the league, who, in a show of solidarity befitting postal employees everywhere, vowed that they would not work the game unless the Devils' coach was punished. When game time rolled around, referee Dave Newell (who was also the referee union leader) and his linesmen steadfastly refused to officiate. Out of desperation, the league called upon a trio of non-union officials (scab refs?) to work the game. The linesmen wore yellow practice jerseys early in the contest, lending a slightly surreal edge to the proceedings. The Devils won that game but were stomped 7-1 in the series-ender, with Schoenfeld sitting the game out due to an *official* one-game suspension. The principals in this conflict have long since resolved their differences, but the legend lives on. This story is indispensable hockey-talk fodder, so now you can nod knowledgeably next time it comes up. And have another donut, while you're at it.

Got $100 Million Burning a Hole in Your Pocket?

Christmas rolls around, and yet again you are stumped as to what to get the man who has everything. Get him another power tool and chances are you'll be driving to the emergency room or calling the insurance company, or both. Look no further, the perfect gift, an NHL franchise of your very own, can be yours for the low, low price of $100 million U.S. That's the kind of up-front money you're going to need to file an application for your very own pro hockey team. You'll also need an arena in which to play and a city in which to build it, staff to run the operation on the ice as well as behind the scenes, minor-league affiliates from which to draw future playing talent, a very large wad of cash with which to pay player salaries, and uh, oh yeah, players. They will come from free-agent acquisitions (players with no contractual obligations to other teams) as well as from the expansion draft in which the other teams in the league are allowed to protect a certain number of players, leaving the rest of their roster free for the picking.

Sounds like a lot of time and effort, doesn't it? Well, look at the bright side, when you assemble thirty or forty strong young men before you at training camp, you can make "try out" mean anything you want ...

Why do the Play-offs Last so Long?

Schedules, Conferences, and Teams

National Hockey League Teams: Whose Side Are You On, Anyway?

The teams in the NHL are divided into two large conferences: the Eastern and the Western. These conferences are further divided. The Eastern Conference has three divisions: Atlantic, Southeast, and Northeast. The Western Conference also has three divisions: Northwest, Pacific, and Central. Like so:

Eastern Conference

Atlantic	Southeast	Northeast
New Jersey	Florida	Boston
N.Y. Islanders	North Carolina	Buffalo
N.Y. Rangers	Tampa Bay	Montreal
Philadelphia	Washington	Ottawa
Pittsburgh	Atlanta	Toronto

Western Conference

Northwest	Pacific	Central
Calgary	Anaheim	Chicago
Colorado	Dallas	Detroit
Edmonton	Los Angeles	St. Louis
Vancouver	Phoenix	Columbus
Minnesota	San Jose	Nashville

bruce:
Personally, I preferred the way the league was divided in the "old days." Why, when I was a lad, we didn't even have divisions, we just etched the names of the teams on the side of a boulder with a sharpened stick, and we liked it!

No, really, the conferences and divisions used to sport the names of legendary hockey figures and regal titles. Take, for example, the Montreal Canadiens. They were in the Adams Division (named after Jack Adams, former coach and GM of the Detroit Red Wings) of the Prince of Wales Conference. Pretty snazzy, eh?

The other conference was named after Clarence Campbell, onetime NHL president, and consisted of the Norris (after James Norris, former owner-president of the Red Wings) and Patrick (after Lester Patrick, longtime coach and GM of the New York Rangers) divisions. The other Wales Conference division was named after Conn Smythe, the former coach, manager, president, and owner-governor of the Toronto Maple Leafs.

The new names are nothing more than geographic indicators. How much pride can be taken from membership in the Northeast Division of the Eastern Conference? It removes all of the mystery and romance, pays no tribute to the rich history of the game. Should can be renamed Northern Area of the North American Continer No, I say, give us back our old names. Add a few more to co expansion, there are plenty of names out there. Richard Conference? Howe Division? Why not?

Teena:
whatever.

The reason for establishing the new divisions in 1998 was to allow for the addition of four new expansion teams. The Nashville Predators joined the Central Division in 1998. Atlanta welcomed the Thrashers for the start of the 1999–2000 season. As the first year of the new millennium draws to a close, the Columbus Blue Jackets and the Minnesota Wild round out the expansion by joining the Central and Northwest divisions, respectively.

What's the Point?

The reason for all this division? The sacred quest of hockey: the battle for the Stanley Cup. Teams compete throughout the season, playing a total of eighty-two games each: half at home, half on the road. For each win, a team is awarded two points. A tie is worth one point, and a loss is, well, a loss. No points there. At the end of the season, points are compared, and the top eight point-getting teams in each conference head for the playoffs. The others head for the golf course.

The conference titles are settled first. Within each conference the first-place team plays the eighth-place team in a best-of-seven series. Likewise, the second-placers play the sevenths, the thirds play the sixths, and the fourths play the fifths. This system rewards the teams who finish higher by pairing them up with the teams that ranked farthest below them. Simply, winning your division guarantees you one of the three top spots in the conference playoffs.

The elimination process proceeds with series winners matching up until only two teams remain, one from each conference. These two will face off in a final seven-game series for the hallowed Stanley Cup (add your own booming-echo voice here). It is impossible for two teams in the same conference to ever meet in the final. Montreal and Ottawa, say, will never fight it out for the cup.

The first two games of each seven-game series are played in the rink of the team that finished with the better record. The venue then switches to the other team's home for the third and fourth. The remaining three games, if necessary, are played alternately. The "home-ice advantage" goes to the team in whose rink the potential series-clinching game will be played. For example, say your team splits the first two games at home and then wins the next two in enemy territory. Now you have the opportunity to win the series on home ice in game five.

So there we have it. After all is said and done, the playoffs could require up to 105 games to produce a championship winner. Despite this almost mind-boggling schedule, once the series starts and you catch the bug, trust me, you'll hate to see it end. Playoff hockey is still the most exciting you're going to see. Regular-season games, with the possible exception of late-season runs for a playoff berth, are a gamble. Sometimes it's end-to-end barn-burning hockey, sometimes it's dump-and-chase, dump-and-chase. There are more than a few players who give considerably less than their all during the regular season. Perhaps a little less cash and a little more fear for their jobs would perk these slug-boys up.

I Used to Be a King, Now I'm Just a Duck: The Teams

NHL team names are an incredibly diverse collection, ranging from the intimidating to the just plain weird. Some conjure up the image of valiant men and women fighting for a noble cause: the Rangers, the Kings. Some call upon the animal kingdom for their strength: the Panthers, the Predators, the Sharks. Even the more powerful of natural phenomena are present: the Hurricane, the Lightning, the Avalanche.

Then, of course, we have the somewhat less intimidating, more mystifying team names. One must assume that these names were chosen by a committee of individuals united by a common lack of understanding of hockey:

- The Senators?: There's an image for you. Twenty-four overweight, overpaid, sedentary politicians trying to organize themselves into a productive unit. Uh-huh. Go team. No, just go, please.
- The Penguins?: Have these people even seen a penguin? Short, stubby legs, useless wings, and fish breath. It's hard to be intimidated by a team named for an animal that looks like one of those inflatable punching-clown toys.
- The Blue Jackets?: Just make sure they never have to play against the Mauve Pumps. They'll clash.
- Finally, the Capitals: Located in Washington, D.C., the Capitals' organization seems to have overlooked some more obvious and more inspiring icons. Hey guys, how about the Presidents? Or maybe the Generals? How about the First Ladies? This just goes to show that the larger the percentage of politicians in the population, the harder even the simplest things become.

Enough about the names, let's take a look at the teams of the NHL. And what an odd bunch they are …

Anaheim Mighty Ducks

– First season: 1993–94
– Stanley Cup wins: 0

In 1992, the Disney Corporation released a movie called *The Mighty Ducks* starring Emilio Estevez. The film followed the adventures of a kids' hockey club that struggled against adversity and, in true Disney fashion, came together to win the big game at the end. The movie grossed close to $60 million. Hmmm, thought Disney, let's release a sequel … and, hey, let's apply for an NHL expansion team too.

What?!

Well, Disney got its franchise (They didn't say no to Disney? I'm shocked) and the Anaheim team began its first NHL season at the Duck Pond. Their debut season brought thirty-three wins, an NHL record for a new team. They also had the most road wins by a new team, at nineteen. Not too shabby for a bunch of guys whose parent company also employs Goofy.

Today, the Ducks boast a roster including Swedish sensation Teemu Selanne and superstar-in-the-making Paul Kariya. As I recall, Donald Duck and his nephews played a pretty mean game of hockey. Donald, I'm afraid, would probably be a goon.

Atlanta Thrashers

– First season: 1999–2000
– Stanley Cup wins: 0

The Atlanta Thrashers join the NHL for the start of the 1999–2000 season. Atlanta hasn't had a team since 1980, when the Flames left town to set up in Calgary. The new team is owned by media mogul Ted Turner (as in Turner Broadcasting; wonder if they'll show any games?) and bears the name of the Georgia state bird, the thrasher.

Boston Bruins

– First season: 1924–25
– Stanley Cup wins: 1929, 1939, 1941, 1970, 1972

Ask any hockey fan to say the first word that comes to mind at the mention of the Boston Bruins and that word will undoubtedly be "Orr." (Unless you ask a Canadiens fan, of course. Then the answer will more commonly be something like "Suck!") Bobby Orr epitomizes the high-water mark of the Boston franchise. He led the team to two Stanley Cup wins, one in 1970 and another in 1972. (For more on Bobby Orr see Chapter 10.)

Most recently, the Bruins shining star was Cam Neely. He was Boston's leading scorer for ten of his seven seasons. In 1996 he was forced to retire due to chronic hip pain. That left Boston in a dreaded "rebuilding phase." That's what team owners say when a team is left in the lurch between retiring veterans and not-quite-ready-for-prime-time players.

Boston has since rebuilt and gotten results from their young players.

Buffalo Sabres

– First season: 1970–71
– Stanley Cup wins: 0

After leading his native land, the Czech Republic, to a gold medal in the 1998 Winter Olympics, goaltender Dominik "The Dominator" Hasek is the undisputed highlight of the Sabres' organization. A two-time Vezina Trophy winner, he is the foundation upon which the Sabres will build their Stanley Cup dreams.

In 1998, the Sabres made a run at the Stanley Cup that left more than a few opponents shaking their heads. No matter how badly the rest of the team faltered, Hasek made magical save after magical save. Buffalo finally fell at the hands of the Washington Capitals in the conference finals. In 1999, the Sabres again made it to the Cup finals but lost in an exciting triple overtime game to the Dallas Stars.

Calgary Flames (Atlanta Flames)

– First season: 1972–73 (Atlanta), 1980–81 (Calgary)
– Stanley Cup win: 1989

In 1980 the Atlanta Flames left home and set up camp in Calgary, keeping their old name in a new town. Atlanta saw NHL action again in 1999, when the Thrashers began play as an expansion franchise.

Calgary is home to the annual celebration of all things cowboy: the Calgary Stampede. The closest the Flames come to cowboydom is having their butts kicked by the Blackhawks. After a Stanley Cup win in 1989, the Flames have spent much of their time trying to fashion (but never quite succeeding) a team that clicks like their predecessors. The leadership of veterans like player Lanny McDonald and coach Bob Johnson is hard to replace.

Carolina Hurricanes (Hartford Whalers)

– First season: 1979–80 (Hartford), 1997–98 (Carolina)
– Stanley Cup wins: 0

In 1997, the beleaguered Hartford Whalers packed up and headed to North Carolina to get a fresh start as the Carolina Hurricanes. A three-year spiral had seen the team lose not only hockey games and fan support but, as a result, over $45 million. Neither a logo and color makeover nor the play of veteran and fan favorite Kevin Dineen could keep the Whalers in Hartford any longer.

Hartford first joined the NHL as part of a team expansion in 1979 that saw four teams (Winnipeg, Quebec, Edmonton, and Hartford) join the ranks after the WHA folded. In their inaugural season, the Whalers were honored with the presence of Gordie Howe. Throughout the 1980s, however, it was Ron Francis who led the team. Traded to Pittsburgh in 1991 (a move many Hartford faithful felt was an unspeakable betrayal by team owners), Francis remains the top dog in most of the club's all-time-scoring categories. The best finish that the Whalers enjoyed was a division title in 1987.

As a final insult to former Whalers fans, the Hurricane reacquired fan favorite Ron Francis in a deal with the Penguins in 1998.

Chicago Blackhawks

– First season: 1926–27
– Stanley Cup wins: 1934, 1938, 1961

Chicago's hockey history combines both talent and innovation. Bobby Hull (aka the Golden Jet) became the first player to score more than 50 goals in a season on his way to a team-record 604. Stan Mikita played for twenty-one glorious years and ranks second to Hull in scoring, with 541. Both players are unofficially credited with inventing the curved blade. Previously, players stickhandled with blades that were board-straight. A curved blade allows more control of the puck.

Columbus Blue Jackets

– First season: 2000–01
– Stanley Cup wins: 0

In 2000, the Blue Jackets will complete a four-team expansion that began in 1998 with the introduction of the Nashville Predators. Columbus and the Minnesota Wild will follow the addition of the Atlanta Thrashers from the previous year.

Colorado Avalanche

– First season: 1979–80 (Quebec), 1995–96 (Colorado)
– Stanley Cup win: 1996

Throughout their tenure in Quebec, the Nordiques were the evil arch-enemy of the Montreal Canadiens. Regardless of where the teams were in the standings, a game between the Nords and the Habs was a fight to the death. "The Battle of Quebec" had as its prize bragging rights that lasted until the next matchup came around.

In 1991, the Quebec Nordiques were granted first pick in the NHL entry draft. Their choice was up-and-coming, hot-commodity, star-of-the-future, franchise-in-a-box, man-of-the-hour Eric Lindros. Only problem was, he didn't want to play for them and demanded to be traded. After much gnashing of teeth and pulling of hair, the Nordiques made a deal with Philadelphia for seven players and a huge chunk of cash. In 1995, the Nordiques were sold and moved to Colorado. They were renamed the Avalanche.

All-star forward Joe Sakic stayed on and was joined by the scrappy Claude Lemieux and super Swede Peter Forsberg. The addition of Patrick Roy in goal was the last piece in the puzzle. Colorado was a solid team top to bottom and steamrolled to the 1996 championship.

Quebec hockey fans are still a little touchy about the whole thing. Best not to talk about it.

Dallas Stars

– First season: 1967–68 (Minnesota), 1993–94 (Dallas)
– Stanley Cup win: 1999

The Dallas Stars were formerly known as the Minnesota North Stars. Earlier in Minnesota, the Stars had merged with the Cleveland Barons. The Barons were formerly the California Seals. Talk about a colorful lineage: "Well, I'm a Star. My father was a North Star; he married a Baron who used to be a Seal."

The North Stars entered the NHL in 1967 and made it to the Stanley Cup final twice, in 1981 and 1991. The first season after their move to Dallas, the Stars collected a meager 66 points; the following year they finished with 104, a franchise record. Last year, the Stars made their first appearance in the Stanley Cup finals and took home the Cup. It looks like shining Star Mike Modano has all the backup he needs to lead his team on another serious charge for the Cup this year.

Detroit Red Wings

– First season: 1926–27 (Cougars), 1930–31 (Falcons),
        1932–33 (Red Wings)
– Stanley Cup wins: 1936, 1937, 1943, 1950, 1952, 1954, 1955, 1997, 1998

In 1995 and 1996, the Red Wings made it to the final, yet failed to deliver the Stanley Cup that their fans expected of them. In 1997, expectations didn't run quite so high, a fact that may have alleviated some of the pressure, allowing Detroit to build momentum through the early rounds and ultimately to sweep the final against Philadelphia. The win ended a forty-two-year drought between championship teams in Detroit, second only to the long-suffering New York Rangers' record of fifty-four.

The winning combination combined the legendary coaching talents of Scotty Bowman, the speed and scoring of stars like Brendan Shanahan and captain Steve Yzerman (sigh), and the all-around domination of the Russian Five: Sergei Fedorov, Igor Larionov, Slava Kozlov, Vladimir Konstantinov, and Viacheslav Fetisov.

The Stanley Cup champion team of 1955 capped a period of Red Wings' domination that saw them win four Stanley Cups in six years. This was the era of Gordie Howe, who held the NHL records for goals and points until his numbers were surpassed by Wayne Gretzky.

Edmonton Oilers

– First season: 1979–80
– Stanley Cup wins: 1984, 1985, 1987, 1988, 1990

No doubt you've heard your hockey guy rant and rave about Wayne Gretzky to the point where you just want him to go live with Wayne if he loves him that much. I'm not going to sing you the "Ballad of Gretzky" here. If you're interested, Bruce and Will go into great detail about the Great One in Chapter 10. I'm here to tell you a little about the Oilers. You know, those other guys who played (and play) in Edmonton.

The Oilers joined the NHL in 1979 as part of the WHA crossover-expansion thing. In five short years, they had assembled a team that would achieve dynasty status in their new league, winning five Cups in seven years. Besides you-know-who, the key players in this grand achievement were men like the intimidating Mark Messier (more on Marky in Chapter 10), swift sniper Jari Kurri, all-around player Glen

Anderson, "not on my watch" defenseman Kevin Lowe, and rock-steady goalie Grant Fuhr.

General Manager Glen "Slats" Sather had and has a knack for selecting young talent and grooming them into solid big-league players. Meanwhile, team owner Peter Pocklington has been widely vilified by the Oilers faithful, not least for his trading of Wayne to Los Angeles in 1988. That trade was the beginning of the end of the Oilers' dominance of the NHL, but look out, Edmonton is beginning to reap the benefits of Sather's savvy selections. A young Oiler team is on the rise again.

Florida Panthers

– First season: 1993–94
– Stanley Cup wins: 0

The Florida Panthers are something of an expansion anomaly. Most expansion teams undergo growing pains for their first couple of seasons, playing hockey that is often painful to watch (witness the toothless Sharks of San Jose's first couple of seasons). But not the Panthers. No, sir. They actually played respectable hockey from the outset. So much so, in fact, that they went all the way to the Cup final in 1996 before being buried by the unstoppable Avalanche.

In their first season, the big cats collected a record eighty-three points as a new team and came very close to making the playoffs. The sharp coaching of Roger Neilson in their early years, combined with standout goaltending courtesy of John Vanbiesbrouck, gave the Panthers a strong foundation upon which to build a successful franchise.

Los Angeles Kings

– First season: 1967–68
– Stanley Cup wins: 0

In their thirty-plus years in the NHL, the Kings have never had the pleasure of reigning over the league as Stanley Cup sovereigns. The closest that they have come was a five game defeat at the hands of the Canadiens in the 1993 Cup final.

The team that found itself in that final was led by none other than Wayne Gretzky. Gretzky spent a few seasons with the Kings before heading to New York via St. Louis. His arrival on the West Coast followed the departure a little more than a year earlier of longtime Kings leader Marcel

Dionne (who, coincidentally, also went East and hooked up with the Rangers). Dionne, a small yet wily center, came to the Kings in the mid-1970s. L.A. was privileged to reap the benefits of 550 of Dionne's 731 career goals, a marker that earns him a third-place standing in the NHL record books.

One additional Kings accomplishment that deserves mention is the wise revamping of their colors. In the 1970s you could spot a King a mile away. Their uniforms were a truly blinding combination of gold and purple, with a big margarine-tub crown on the chest. Regal? Perhaps. Tasteful? No. The modern color scheme of black, white, and silver may not be as eye-catching, but at least now the Kings aren't *always* painful to watch.

Minnesota Wild

– First season: 2000–01
– Stanley Cup wins: 0

The millennium will see NHL hockey action return to Minnesota for the first time since the North Stars left town in 1994. As with the expansion teams mentioned previously, there's not much one can say about the Wild at this point. I'm not going to let that stop me this time, however. Who wants to read another "The [team name goes here] will begin play in blah blah blah blah ..." section, right?

If I were a politician, I might feel confident expounding the virtues of an as yet unseen and untried future venture. I suspect it would go something like this:

"My friends, let me tell you this, if there is one thing upon which you can depend it is that players will come and players will go, goals will be scored and penalties will be taken, sometimes in our favor and sometimes against us, but make no mistake, when time has run out and goals are tallied, one team will be victorious and one team will be vanquished and, my friends, I promise you today that when one of those teams moves forward in victory whilst the other languishes in defeat, our very own Minnesota Wild will be one of those teams, of that we can be certain!"

There is also one other thing of which I am certain—well, two things actually. One is that when the music coordinator at the Wild's home rink wants to rally the crowd behind the team, he or she will undoubtedly play, you guessed it, "Wild Thing." And second, by the time the 2000–01 season comes to a close, we will all be sick of that damn song.

Montreal Canadiens

– First season: 1917–18
– Stanley Cup wins: 24

1916, 1924, 1930, 1931, 1944, 1946,
1953, 1956, 1957, 1958, 1959, 1960,
1965, 1966, 1968, 1969, 1971, 1973,
1976, 1977, 1978, 1979, 1986, 1993!

> **Teena:**
> Are you happy now?

> **Bruce:**
> Yes, thanks. (Go Habs Go!)

> **Will:**
> oh just get on with it already!

How, you may ask, did the Canadiens win their first Stanley Cup Championship in 1916 if their first season was in 1917? Good question. The answer lies in the Stanley Cup. This trophy-among-trophies was first given in 1893 as a reward for a first-place finish in the Amateur Hockey Association of Canada. The first time the Montreal club won the Cup as the Canadiens was 1916. The NHL didn't come into existence until 1917.

One thing is for sure, the Canadiens laid claim to the Cup early in their history and were reluctant to let it go from that moment on. They hold the record, not only for most championships ever, with twenty-four, but also for most consecutive Cup wins, with five (1956–60). The Toronto Maple Leafs are a distant second in all-time wins, with thirteen.

The roster of past Montreal players reads like a who's who of the Hall of Fame. Greats like Maurice "The Rocket" Richard, Ken Dryden, Jean Beliveau, Jacques Plante, Guy Lafleur and Larry Robinson are but a few of the players who brought home Lord Stanley's Cup time and time again.

> **Bruce:**
> would just like to point out to fans of lesser teams (i.e., the oilers) that the Canadiens are the only team in the league to have won at least one Stanley Cup Championship (and as many as six) every decade since this century was in its teens.

> The only team that is even remotely close in all-time Cup wins (the Leafs, with thirteen) has not won a Cup in over thirty years. The Canadiens' organization is simply the winningest team in the history of the NHL.

> P.S. The Canadiens' parent company is a brewery (Molson). The oilers were owned by a guy who runs a wiener factory.

Nashville Predators

– First season: 1998–99
– Stanley Cup wins: 0

Nashville had a typically bad first season, not the worst in the league, though. They tallied twenty-eight wins, forty-seven losses, and seven ties.

New Jersey Devils

– First season: 1974–75 (Kansas City Scouts), 1976–77 (Colorado Rockies),
        1982–83 (New Jersey Devils)
– Stanley Cup win: 1995

The Devils began life as Scouts. (What does that say about the Scouting movement?) The Scouts followed a disastrous first couple of seasons in Kansas with a move to Colorado, a name change (Rockies), and a disastrous six seasons in Denver. Never the type to rest on their laurels, the Rockies pulled up stakes and moved to New Jersey under the orders of new owner John McMullen in 1982. Things were pretty much business as usual in their new home. After pounding the Devils 11-4 in a 1983 game, Edmonton Oiler Wayne Gretzky, arguably the nicest guy in the league, assessed the Jersey team as a "Mickey Mouse" operation. Gretzky came to regret those words. As the Devils improved, fans donned mouse ears for Oiler visits and rained abuse on Number 99.

The Devils of recent years have put their checkered past behind them. So much so that they swept a Cup-hungry Detroit team in the 1995 final to capture a franchise first Stanley Cup Championship. Under the tutelage of coach Jacques Lemaire (who, incidently, resigned after the high-ranked Devils bowed out of the playoffs in the first round in 1998), the Devils perfected the "neutral-zone trap," a strategy that clogs the neutral zone and stymies the offense of the opposition. The trap can make for slow, low-scoring hockey and has as many detractors as devotees.

The defensive-minded New Jersey team frustrates opponents not only with smothering defensive play, but with the stingy goaltending of Martin Brodeur. Brodeur is one of the NHL's few scoring goalies; he cadged an empty-netter against the Canadiens in the 1997 playoffs.

New York Islanders

– First season: 1972–73
– Stanley Cup wins: 1980, 1981, 1982, 1983

The New York Islanders were a force to be reckoned with in the early 1980s. With the front-line scoring wizardry of Mike Bossy and Bryan Trottier, the strong defensive play of Denis Potvin and the take-no-prisoners aggressive goaltending style of Billy Smith, the Islanders began a dynasty-in-the-making charge that saw them take four straight Stanley Cup Championships home to Long Island. Not only did they displace the Montreal Canadiens as the league's biggest threat, they came within three wins of tying the Canadiens' record of five straight Cup wins. After sweeping the Edmonton Oilers to take their fourth in 1983, the Isles saw their "drive for five" stalled at four by a Gretzky-led Oilers squad the very next year.

New York Rangers

– First season: 1926–27
– Stanley Cup wins: 1928, 1933, 1940, 1994

If there's one thing that the New York Rangers have in abundance, it is patience. After an impressive debut, capturing the Stanley Cup in only their second season of operation and two more in the next twelve years, the Rangers settled in for a long, loooong, wait. It was to be fifty-four years before they had the chance once again to bask in the glow of Lord Stanley's Cup. They did manage to reach the final in 1978, a scant thirty-eight years later, but fell to the mighty Canadiens.

The Rangers team that broke that drought was led by a former Edmonton Oiler who was no stranger to championship celebrations: tower of power Mark Messier. Messier played for New York for six seasons, long enough to win the Cup and have the chance to reunite with friend and longtime teammate Wayne Gretzky. Gretzky was in L.A. when Messier and his mates landed the Ranger's fourth Cup. Messier has since moved on to the West Coast and now scares opponents for the Vancouver Canucks, the team that he personally beat with the game-seven winning goal for that 1994 championship.

Ottawa Senators

– First season: 1992–93*
– Stanley Cup wins: 0

The asterisk beside the first season of play for the Senators indicates that, although the present incarnation of the Ottawa team began operation in 1992, there existed in the early days of the NHL another Senators team based in Canada's capital city. The Senators of yore played from 1917 to 1934 and played well, winning better than 53 percent of their matches. "So what?" I hear you say. Well, consider this: barely a quarter of today's active teams can boast a better record.

At first it seemed that the Senators of today had inherited very little from their ancestral teammates. Ottawa was a threat to nobody but themselves early on. It wasn't until the 1997 playoffs, a competition that saw the Sens advance for the first time, that other teams realized that they wouldn't have Ottawa to kick around anymore. A first-round upset of the first-place New Jersey Devils in the 1998 playoffs served notice that Ottawa was ready to do some kicking of their own.

Philadelphia Flyers

– First season: 1967–68
– Stanley Cup wins: 1974, 1975

The Flyers of the seventies were known as "The Broad Street Bullies." If a fast, play-making team can be likened to a cat burglar creeping silently through the darkness to rob you blind before you realize what is happening, then Philadelphia was an abrasive mugger working in broad daylight. They walked in, beat the hell out of you, and took what they wanted. Seeing file photos of Flyers favorites like Bobby Clarke and Dave "The Hammer" Schultz, I wonder if the team could muster a full set of teeth among them.

Pummeling the competition into submission is only half of the job, though. Somebody has to pick their way through the fallen bodies and put the puck in the net. Philadelphia had that covered too, with players like fifty-goal-scorers Rick MacLeish and Reggie Leach. At the other end of the rink Conn Smythe Trophy winner Bernie Parent kept the rubber out of the Flyers' net.

Today Philly's hopes for the future lie squarely on the shoulders of Eric Lindros. A four-game defeat in the 1997 Cup Final and an embarrassing first-round exit at the hands of Buffalo in 1998 has Flyer faithfuls shaking their heads. Rule changes in late 1998 discouraging obstruction seemed to handcuff a Philadelphia team that had banked heavily on size and strength to carry their playoff hopes.

Phoenix Coyotes

– First season: 1979–80 (Winnipeg Jets), 1996–97 (Phoenix Coyotes)
– Stanley Cup wins: 0

The Phoenix Coyotes rose from the ashes of the Winnipeg Jets in 1996. The former Jets of Winnipeg hadn't exactly gone down in a blaze of glory. During their seventeen NHL years in Manitoba, they had kind of maintained a continuous smolder which threatened, with varying degrees of intensity, to blaze to life at any moment … or not. I don't want to upset any former Jets boosters here, but hey, one of the notable highlights of their tenure in Winnipeg was a club record forty-three wins and ninety-six points in 1984–85.

Not that the Jets were without talented players, at least temporarily. For the first eighteen games of their existence, their roster boasted the scoring talents of Bobby Hull. Then he was traded to Hartford. The all-time team leader in scoring and points was 1981 number-one draft pick Dale Hawerchuk.

In Phoenix, however, things are looking up, relatively speaking. Now on board are fifty-two-goal-man Keith Tkachuk and goalie-on-the-rise Nikolai Khabibulin (Hah-bee-BOO-lin, fun huh?). The Coyotes saw playoff action in 1997 and 1998 but made hasty exits both years.

Pittsburgh Penguins

– First season: 1967–68
– Stanley Cup wins: 1991, 1992

There were three key factors that lead to the Penguins' meteoric rise from league laugh to Stanley Cup stardom in the early nineties. They are, in order of importance: (1) Mario, (2) Mario, and (3) Mario.

Sports Illustrated published a special edition devoted entirely to Mario Lemieux's farewell. It fell just short of a religious text. Stats that I can't believe anyone would care about were documented with loving detail. Mario's last shift, Mario's last point, Mario's last shot. I don't know why they stopped there. How about Mario's last Men's room visit? I can see it now:

Reporter:	*Tell us Mario, as you stepped up to the urinal as number 66 for the last time, what were your thoughts?*
Lemieux:	*Well, to tell the truth, before I went in there, I was feeling pretty anxious. But then, as I stood there knowing that this was the last time I'd take a whiz in the Igloo, a calm came over me suddenly. I was totally at ease. I knew right there that I had done the right thing.*
Reporter:	*Thanks Mario, any thoughts on which one of your teammates will be stepping up to take your place?*
Lemieux:	*Huh?*

I'm not here to mock Mario, however. He was indeed one of the best players who ever laced 'em up, as they say. For far more information than you could possibly want about Super Mario, turn to Bruce's paean to this hockey immortal in Chapter 10. For a more detailed chronicle of Lemieux from diapers to defense, seek out that *S.I.* issue. Your hockey guy probably has it double-bagged and vacuum-sealed, tucked away with his most valuable possessions.

The rest of the Penguins have had to struggle bravely on without their retired teammate. Unlike the Oilers of the 1980s, the Pens have yet to prove that they can do it without their superstar (the Oilers captured another Stanley Cup after The Great Gretzky moved on). The man to watch, and not only for his Euro-Sweetie good looks, is Jaromir Jagr. A dazzling playmaker and scoring threat, Jagr will be the one the Penguins look to as they work to build a Cup contender once more. For a fascinating up-close look at this Czech cutie, turn to my handsome player top ten in Chapter 10.

San Jose Sharks

– First season: 1991–92
– Stanley Cup wins: 0

The Sharks revitalized the team merchandising business with snazzy black-and-white-on-teal away uniforms and snappy logo en route to a 17-

58-5 (Win-Loss-Tie) record in their inaugural season. Oddly, and perhaps sadly, this was no accident. After more than a year of market research went into designing the logo, "sports experts" from Neiman Marcus and Bloomingdale's were consulted on color choice. The hot color for the nineties, Sharks brass were told, was teal. Set it off with black and even the men will go for it.

It worked. Anticipated earnings for the 1993–94 season from the sale of official licensed Sharks merchandise were in excess of $200 million.

"But what about the team, are they any good?" I hear you cry.

Did I mention the teal-on-black San Jose Sharks Durable Polyurethane Lunch Box with optional Big Gulp Shark Attack Inflatable Thermos Pool Float?

Okay, okay, the team. Well, y'know, bad news there, I'm afraid. You see, sharks are more accustomed to warmer water; put them on ice and they tend to flop and thrash around in a fairly threatening manner and yet not really accomplish much. See where I'm going with this?

Actually, it's not as bleak as all that. Despite spending much of their time swimming around in the basement of their division, the Sharks have inflicted a few nasty bites on the competition of late. Having qualified for the post-season for the first time in 1994, San Jose clipped the much-favored Red Wings in a tension-filled seven games. Again in 1995, the Sharks gobbled (!) their opponents, the Calgary Flames, in seven. Both years they failed to advance past the second round, however. In 1998 playoff hopes loomed again only to come crashing down to earth after six games against the Dallas Stars.

St. Louis Blues

– First season: 1967–68
– Stanley Cup wins: 0

The Blues distinguished themselves by making it to the Stanley Cup finals each of their first three years of existence. They did not however, distinguish themselves any further, losing two to Montreal and the third to Boston. They haven't earned a trip to the finals since.

Of late, the Blues have suffered from a kind of "revolving-door syndrome." Under former coach Mike Keenan, all but two Blues were traded over a period of two and a half years.

In 1997–98 the Blues were touted as the "dark horse" of the Stanley Cup race. They trounced the lowly L.A. Kings in four games before falling to the Cup-bound Detroit Red Wings.

Tampa Bay Lightning

– First season: 1992–93
– Stanley Cup wins: 0

It was with the Tampa Bay Lightning that a young goaltender named Manon Rheaume made NHL history. Total NHL playing experience for Rheaume: twenty minutes in a pre-season exhibition game. Why is this history? Because Manon is a woman, the only woman to have ever played pro hockey in the all-male NHL.

The Lightning struck for a playoff spot at the end of the 1995–96 season but failed to advance. They have yet to strike twice. Coach Terry Crisp hung in there as Tampa's fearless leader for the first five years until a less than electrifying 1997 debut saw him handed his walking papers by GM Phil Esposito. NHL veteran coach Jacques Demers stepped in too late to salvage a winning season, and the Tampa Bay team continued their downward slide.

Toronto Maple Leafs

– First season: 1917–18
– Stanley Cup wins: 1918, 1922, 1932, 1942, 1945, 1947, 1948, 1949, 1951, 1962, 1963, 1964, 1967

Bruce: Yeah, yeah. Who cares?

Bruce: Ha! Is that all they've won?

Will: Give it up

Bruce: Do we really need to know this?

The Toronto Maple Leafs rank number two on the list of hockey's all-time superpowers, having iced thirteen Cup champion teams to Montreal's twenty-four. In the NHL's first fifty years, players like King Clancy, Turk Broda, and Howie Meeker made the Leafs a force to be reckoned with, and the Stanley Cup spent most of its time in either Toronto, Montreal, or Detroit.

In the years since 1967, however, the Cup has worked in Toronto (at the Hockey Hall of Fame) but lives elsewhere. Toronto hasn't seen a Cup final series since that 1967 win against Montreal. This despite the outstanding play of club members like Darryl Sittler, Borje Salming, Wilf Paiement, Rick Vaive, and Wendell Clark. Former Leafs owner, the late Harold Ballard, was outstanding in his own right but for a very different reason. Never shy about voicing his opinion on anyone and anything, Ballard distinguished himself as a grumpy old man of the first order. He once called CBC broadcaster Barbara Frum "a dumb broad" and then told her to shut up. He threatened to bar Bobby Hull from Maple Leaf Gardens after Hull suggested that he might remove some of his hockey memorabilia from the Hall of Fame. Under direct questioning by Hull, he denied it.

Hull may have gotten even later. During the pre-game skate at a Leafs–Blues game at the Gardens, Hull took a warmup shot that went over the glass, into Ballard's private box, through his newspaper, and into his nose. Oops, sorry Harry.

When Darryl Sittler was a newcomer to the Leafs, Ballard regarded him as a father's pride and joy. Months later Sittler was, in Ballard's estimation, "a cancer" on the team.

For a guy who believed so strongly in the Hall of Fame that he would bar a player from his rink, Ballard committed what could be the ultimate sin against the history of the game. When famed broadcaster Foster "He Shoots, He Scores!" Hewitt's broadcast booth was removed to allow for the installation of new box seats, it went to the dumpster instead of the Hall of Fame. A public outcry was answered with twenty-five faux Foster chairs (allegedly salvaged from the booth) sold, with the proceeds to go to charity. Each chair was supposed to be Foster's favorite. Foster never had a favorite chair. Harold Ballard. Nice guy.

The 1999 season brought hope to the Leafs; they played well, making the playoffs. It also brought the closing of Maple Leaf Gardens. On Feb. 13 Toronto hosted their last game in the Gardens against the Chicago Blackhawks. It was a poetic closing. The Blackhawks had been the first team to play against Toronto at the opening of the building in 1931. Both times Chicago beat Toronto, first 2-1 and, finally, an embarrassing 6-2.

Vancouver Canucks

– First season: 1970–71
– Stanley Cup wins: 0

The 1997 Vancouver Canucks began the season with a new, make that *another* new, logo. Of late it has been the fashion in the NHL to revitalize your team (or at least your team's merchandising revenue) with a hip, new logo. Vancouver is an old pro at new logo designs. With the advent of the new stylized orca in the shape of a "C," they don the fourth official symbol in their twenty-seven years in the league. Far and away the worst of the bunch were the dayglo-yellow superhero "V" sweaters of the mid-1980s. The new orca is no random animal selection; the team is owned by Orca Bay Sports and Entertainment.

Also new to the team in 1997 was former Oiler great Mark Messier. He joined sniper Alexander Mogilny and gritty team captain Trevor Linden as Vancouver attempted to build a team that could make it to the finals once more (as they had in 1981 and 1994). The parts were assembled, but the Canucks failed to click as they missed the playoffs for the second year in a row.

Washington Capitals

– First season: 1974–75
– Stanley Cup wins: 0

Speaking of new logos, the Capitals' "screaming eagle" crest recently replaced the somewhat dull "Capitals" with a hockey stick as the "L" and a sprinkling of stars. A new, alternate logo depicts the famous dome of the Capitol Building in Washington looming over the team name and a pair of crossed sticks, and a puck. I think we've got the picture, thanks. After setting long-standing NHL records for futility in their early years (fewest points, most goals against, longest losing streak), the Caps have fashioned a team that deserves respect. The 1997–98 incarnation went all the way to the Stanley Cup final a year after missing the post-season for the first time in fifteen years. Unfortunately, their opponents were the somewhat otherworldly, ultimately motivated defending champion Detroit Red Wings. Still, Washington has built a contender with the likes of sharp-shooter Peter Bondra, shaggy tough guy Chris Simon, and always scrappy Dale Hunter. We are likely to hear more from this team in the future.

So Who Was Stanley Anyway?

Hockey's Holy Grail

To the right is a photograph of the glorious Stanley Cup, a trophy awarded every year to the best team in the NHL. As a trained silversmith and jeweler, I find the design intriguing: a small, decorative base with a wide-mouthed goblet on top. Aesthetically, it is an odd, yet appealing, arrangement, one which seems to—*I know, I know*. The picture is upside down. Consider it a test of your hockey-fan status; if you looked at the photo and saw nothing unusual, you are a true neophyte. (Check out your friends. Show them this picture and see if they notice anything unusual.)

Prior to my Saul-like conversion to The Game, I had only ever seen the Stanley Cup in newspaper photos as it was held aloft by some sweaty, unshaven, gap-toothed hockey player. I assumed—and remember, I am a trained, accredited silversmith—that the small end of the trophy went down. I mentioned this to Will, and he was aghast.

"But—but, it's the Stanley Cup," he said, as though that settled everything.

"So?"

"So," he replied. *"It's the Stanley Cup.* It's not just any trophy. It's the Holy Grail. The silver chalice of the hockey gods. *La coupe Stanley.* It's probably the only thing besides beer that both French and English

Canadians are willing to die for."

I shrugged. "I still think it looks better the other way round."

It's true. The Stanley Cup is far more aesthetically pleasing standing on the wrong end. The proper way up, it looks, well, ridiculous. A delicate cup atop a huge, ungainly stand: it's like perching a diamond on a tree trunk. The cup is unbalanced, clunky, awkward, goofy-looking. Now, I realize that describing the Stanley Cup that way smacks of sacrilege, but in all honesty——

> Will:
> Pay her no heed! She's spouting gibberish.
> The Stanley cup is a fine and noble trophy, strong, masculine and–dare I say–phallic. England has her mace and crown, Japan her sword and mirror, but in North America the highest emblem of glory made manifest–the apogee of the apex of the pinnacle of the peak of all that is good and noble and pure in the land–is, well, a hockey trophy. But, oh, what a trophy! It looks–it looks … well, like a tin-plated telescope. But it has personality. And it fair oozes with history and hi-jinx. The Stanley cup goofy-looking? Never!

The Amazing Stupendous Growing Trophy! (Just Add Water)

The Stanley Cup didn't always look so goofy. It began life as a fine-crafted silver bowl with a gold interior finish. So what happened? Why this transformation? The reason is actually quite inspiring. The Stanley Cup is, above all, a player's trophy. Unique among professional sports awards, the Stanley Cup is engraved, not only with the names of the winning teams, but with the names of *all* the players on *each* winning team.

It began as graffiti, with players scratching their names onto the Cup (it was soft silver and easily marked; you can still see some of the names scratched on the original). This early tradition soon became official policy, and the players' names were engraved on a silver band and added to the base. As time went by, the engravers ran out of space and more rings were added, making it the only sports trophy that *grows*. It keeps getting bigger and bigger, and harder to move as the years go by—kind of like hubby.

The Stanley Cup

Meet Lord Stanley

Yes, there really was a Stanley. None other than Lord Frederick Arthur Stanley (1842–1908), the son of a British prime minister, a one time member of British Parliament, and a peer of the House of Lords. How did a pedigreed Englishman such as this become associated with the brawn and brawl of professional ice hockey? Two reasons: (1) he was a fan, and (2) he was a big-wig, the Queen's representative in Canada, Governor General of the Dominion.

Lord Stanley arrived in Canada in 1888 amid all the usual pomp and ceremony, but at heart he was just a regular guy. Which is to say, a sports nut. Although he had never seen a hockey game before his arrival, he soon became enamored with the game. Lord Stanley was an energetic man in more ways than one: he had no fewer than ten children: eight sons and two daughters. Soon the entire family was strapping on skates and whacking a puck around. Even Lady Stanley got into the act.

The Cup

As more and more hockey clubs formed, rivalries began, teams acquired patrons, and stars appeared. All that was missing was a unified trophy. Other trophies did exist, some of them quite grand, but in the 1800s trophies were fought for permanently. That is, if a club won any given trophy three years in a row, they got to keep it. Often, elaborate silver trophies would be taken out of circulation because of this.

Lord Stanley wanted a trophy that would be fought for annually, one that would never be won permanently, one that would promote amateur hockey as a whole. And so, in 1893, Stanley sent to London, England, for a trophy.

What he received was a silver bowl, 7 ½ inches high and 11 ½ inches across, with gold-finish interior set atop an ebony base. It was designed for displaying roses. Where other hockey trophies were garish, Stanley's bowl was understated and dignified. (Although sportswriter D'Arcy Jenish describes the original squat bowl as having "possessed all the grace and stature of a soup tureen.") It cost the then princely sum of ten guineas, the equivalent of $48.66.

An Inauspicious Start

The Montreal Amateur Athletic Association (MAAA) had the best record in 1893, so they were simply handed the trophy. It wasn't until the following year that the first real Stanley Cup game was played. The MAAA defended their title as the Stanley Cup team—and won. They were now in a position to win it a third straight time and take permanent ownership. This, of course, was not what Lord Stanley had in mind. Talk about a waste; the Cup would have disappeared from competition only three years after it was donated.

When the MAAA was told that no matter how many times they won the Cup they would never get to keep it, they got cranky and said, "Fine! Who needs your damn Cup anyway." After all, the MAAA had already won permanent possession of a much larger and far more elaborate trophy. It was only after extended negotiations that the MAAA finally condescended to take Stanley's trophy. That's right, there was a time you couldn't give the Stanley Cup away.

A Rose by Any Other Name

Lord Stanley's trophy was originally called the Dominion Hockey Challenge Cup (this is the name you still see engraved across it). For a while it was called Stanley's Rose Bowl, and later the Stanley Challenge Trophy, but over time it became known as the Stanley Cup, first in nickname and later officially. Today, most fans and players are on a first-name basis, referring to it simply as "Stanley." It is the oldest professional sports trophy awarded anywhere in North America.

Royalty on Ice

Ironically, Lord Stanley never got to watch a single Stanley Cup game. He was recalled to Britain shortly after he donated the trophy and he never visited Canada again. He did not, however, give up on hockey. He even tried to introduce it to England, and in 1895 he captained a team with four of his sons in an exhibition bout against the Royal household on a frozen pond behind Buckingham Palace. The Stanley Family team pummeled the royals, scoring one goal after another. The Palace Team included two future kings: the Prince of Wales (later, Edward the VII) and the Duke of York (later, George the V).

The Other Stanley Cup

That's right, there is another Stanley Cup. After returning to England, the Stanley family later donated another trophy—one for race-car driving. So if you want to sound really hip and knowledgeable, the next time some hockey fanatic is going on about the Stanley Cup, ask blithely but with a knowing half-smile, "To which Stanley Cup are you referring?"

Overtime Interruptus: The Sabbath Rules!

Early Stanley Cup games were marked by oddities and troubles: arenas where the roofs were so poorly put together that snow drifted through during games; ice surfaces with holes so deep that pucks occasionally disappeared; dogs that ran out and stole the puck in mid-game; and, even more exasperating, religious-minded officials who took exception to games played on the Sabbath. Imagine a high-pitched exciting Saturday night game, tied 2-2 and going into overtime. The players are flying, the fans are crazed, the excitement is mounting … Suddenly, Cinderella-like, at the stroke of midnight the game ends. The mayor steps out and orders all activity to cease. At one minute after midnight it is now officially Sunday and no games will be allowed. This actually happened in Westmount, Quebec, back when going to church was considered more important than hockey. If you can imagine such a thing.

Hockey's Challengers

Today, Stanley is awarded to the best team in the NHL, following a very long playoff that includes the semi-finals, finals, division championships, more finals, and finally the final finals, all of which actually takes longer than the regular season to complete. (I'm kidding of course. It only *feels* that way.)

It was much simpler in the early years, when Stanley was a challenge trophy. Whichever team held the Cup had to fend off direct challenges for it, sometimes several in a year. The Montreal Wanderers, for example, defeated four different teams in 1908. The challenge system finally ended in 1927, when the NHL consolidated control over the Stanley Cup and introduced a playoff system.

Manly Names to Strike Terror in the Hearts of opponents

The challenge era included a dizzying array of teams. Among my favorites: the Creamery Kings, the Rosebuds, the Canaries, and the Quakers. That's right, the Quakers.

What's next? The Fightin' Amish?

The Ballad of the Dawson Nuggets

The most bizarre challenge of all, however, occurred in 1904, when a band of gold miners and government clerks from the far arctic reaches of the Yukon traveled to Ottawa to fight for the right to Stanley. The journey was an epic, 3,800-mile (6,400-km) trek that involved everything from dogsleds and snowshoes, to steamships and steam locomotives.

Dawson City was a wild northern boom town, born of the Klondike gold rush, and a millionaire promoter named Colonel Joe Boyle decided to put together a hockey team. The colonel had made a fortune in the Klondike by running prospectors through the notorious Whitehorse rapids and parlaying this into a lumber empire. He was known as the "King of the Klondike." The colonel issued his Stanley Cup challenge to the Ottawa Silver Seven. A matchup like that, he said, would be "a hockey promoter's dream." Instead, it turned into a nightmare.

Colonel Boyle's team, the Dawson City Nuggets, was an odd mix of teenagers and oldtimers. One of the team members had played pro hockey back in Ottawa; others had barely played at all. No matter, funded by their extravagant benefactor they set out on what would become a legendary journey. It began on December 19, 1904. They traveled from Dawson to Whitehorse on snowshoes and dogsled. Some even attempted to bicycle it, but were forced to give up.

Trapped by a blizzard in Whitehorse, they eventually crossed the mountains into Skagway, Alaska, where the temperature had dropped to –48°F (chilly -44°C). They missed their ship and had to wait five days in Skagway before catching a steamer out. Severe fog forced the ship further south than they wanted to go, and the team had to disembark in Seattle and then travel north back to Vancouver. From Vancouver they took a bone-wearying transcontinental train across North America. After twenty-three grueling days on the road, they finally came limping into Ottawa.

They were worn out and exhausted, plagued by frostbite and fatigue, and no sooner had they arrived that they were told, "Suit up, boys!" The first game was scheduled for the following evening.

Colonel Boyle protested and asked for a few days for his team to recuperate, but the Ottawa backers—in a mean-spirited move—refused. The Dawson players had to scramble to buy equipment and prepare for the opening bout.

The series began, appropriately enough for the Nuggets, on Friday the 13th. The Dawson team was trounced 9 to 2. One of the Dawson players made the mistake of saying that the Ottawa star player, Frank McGee, hadn't looked all that hot. The Ottawa fans, meanwhile, began grumbling that the Ottawa players had gone too easy on the Dawson boys.

What followed was closer to a massacre than a hockey game. The Silver Seven vowed to redeem themselves, and Frank McGee came out flying. The game was a real cliffhanger. Ottawa just squeaked by with a narrow 23-to-2 victory. (The Nuggets' strategy, you see, was to let the Ottawa players tire themselves out firing pucks into their net and then strike back.)

Frank McGee, the one-eyed wonder and future Hall of Famer, scored fourteen goals in that final game, a record that still stands, and probably will until the Yukon comes up with another team. McGee did it not just with one eye, but with a broken wrist as well. At one point he scored three goals in ninety seconds.

The Dawson Nuggets straggled home and Frank McGee basked in what would be short-lived glory. He was dead at the age of thirty-seven.

When the First World War began, Frank McGee, burning with patriotic fervor, signed up for the army. Although blind in one eye and thus exempt from service, Frank managed to conceal his handicap and bluffed his way into the army. He was killed in action in a muddy field in France.

Hockey Goes Pro

It wasn't long before hockey turned professional. In 1908, the Ottawa Senators—already a hockey legend—became the first wholly professional hockey team in Canada, and the strategy paid off; they won the Stanley Cup the following season, and went on to take it five more times. The Silver Seven, as they were known, was hockey's first great dynasty. (They were also known for their red, white, and black stripped turtleneck sweaters, which earned them another nickname: "The Barber Poles.")

A common misconception is that the Stanley Cup was donated solely for amateur hockey. This isn't exactly true. Lord Stanley never mentioned amateur teams specifically, it was just assumed. It was, however, strictly designated as a trophy for the top *Canadian* team. But it didn't take long for the United States to field a championship team.

When an American team from the Pacific League first challenged for the Cup, there was a nationalistic uproar in Canada. Lord Stanley had donated the trophy for Canadians, they declared. We couldn't let foreign-based teams snatch it away. But the Cup's trustees squashed the objections. In a reinterpretation of Lord Stanley's original decree, they decided: "The Stanley Cup represents more than the championship of Canada. It's really the symbol of the championship of the world." Except of course, it never did become a world cup, but only a North American one. In 1917, the Seattle Mets became the first American hockey team to win the Stanley Cup. They wouldn't be the last.

The Year Stanley Got Sick

The Stanley Cup has been awarded every year since 1893 except once. It happened in 1919 at the height of a worldwide influenza epidemic that killed millions of people. One of the victims was also—ironically—one of the strongest, healthiest players in hockey. During a hard-fought Stanley Cup series between Montreal and Seattle, Joe Hall, a star player, skated to the bench and collapsed. A few days later, Hall died and the series was canceled. The Stanley Cup was not awarded, and public gatherings as a whole were actively discouraged. (Years later, during the players' strike of 1992, the Stanley Cup finals once again came within a hair's breadth of being canceled, but at the last minute a compromise was worked out.)

Insults Galore

As the saga of the Dawson Nuggets suggests, the Stanley Cup has faced its share of ignominy over the years. Remember: for all its cult-icon appeal, the Stanley Cup is still a *hockey* trophy, and hockey is a game played—predominantly—by hockey players. And not just any kind of hockey players, but usually *Canadian* hockey players. This is a group of people who took until 1959 (!) to figure out that they should probably put masks on their goaltenders.

Now, consider giving, even temporarily, an antique silver cup to people like these (i.e., Canadian hockey players) and you can imagine the outcome. Lord Stanley's Cup has been dented, lost, misplaced, stolen, used to serve up dog food, and even, well, pooped into—by a baby and an adult (I won't get into the who and why of that last item, except to point out that the player responsible was born in England and therefore was not, technically, a Canadian. No red-blooded [adult] Canuck would dream of such desecration. Check *Pride & Glory* by William Houston for the rest of the details.)

What follows then is a mere sampling of what can happen when you let hockey players near a valuable silver bowl.

Drop-Kicked!

In 1905, the Ottawa Silver Seven won the Stanley Cup. As a band of drunken players staggered home from a victory celebration, the talk turned to football. (Several of the players were active in both sports.) An academic point arose, one dealing with aerodynamics and skill, namely: "I wonder how far a person could drop-kick the Stanley Cup." This is the type of question that athletes—especially drunken, male athletes—take quite seriously.

And so, on a dare, one of them gave it a shot. At that time, no collars had been added to it and Stanley was still a small cup, not much bigger than a football. The player did an admirable job, and the Stanley Cup flew gracefully through the air, disappearing into the Rideau Canal, which was—fortunately—frozen at that time. The players cheered, and congratulations were offered all round, and they crawled off to bed.

Only later, when officials asked for the Cup (it was due to be engraved), did the players see the error of their ways. One of the players, Harry Smith, went hustling back to the Rideau Canal and, after a frantic search, found it lodged in the snow, where it had landed. It was whisked back to the engraver just in time.

Stanley—Abandoned!

In 1924, the Montreal Canadiens won the Stanley Cup, and all the usual ingredients were in place for further misadventures: drunken hockey players, wild celebrations, and a valuable silver trophy. (Note to the NHL: These items don't mix well.)

The team owner had invited the players back to his house for further celebrations, and a carload of hockey players piled into a Model T with

the Cup in tow and went roaring down the street. Unfortunately, they blew a tire. Fortunately, the players piled out of the car and were able to change the tire in no time. Unfortunately, they forgot the Stanley Cup during their excited he-man activities.

Off they drove, leaving Stanley sitting by the curb. When they arrived at the party, festivities were in full swing and it was only when the owner proposed to fill the Cup with champagne that they noticed it was missing.

Once again, an embarrassed hockey player was sent scrambling to retrieve hockey's pride and joy. (All I can say is, it's a good thing these hockey players weren't put in charge of watching a baby, or even a pet.)

Geraniums Anyone?

The canal was only the beginning. Stanley later suffered the ultimately humiliation: being converted into a flower pot. It happened after the Cup went home with the victorious Montreal Wanderers in 1907. Proud to have captured hockey's greatest trophy, the players took the Cup out for a commemorative photo—and promptly forgot it at the studio. By the time anyone noticed it was missing, several months had passed and the photographer's wife had planted lovely red geraniums in it. (Though, I wonder how much truth there is in this tale; one version has it happening to the Silver Seven in 1905, another source says it happened to the Wanderers—in 1908. But why let fact spoil a wonderful story?)

Playing Injured

If you want to understand the grip that the Stanley Cup has on players, you need look no further than Bobby "Not a Rocket Scientist" Baun of the Toronto Maple Leafs. In the 1964 finals, Bobby broke his leg. Now, normally this would signal a trip to the hospital, or at least the dressing room. But not with the Stanley Cup on the line. Bobby had his leg wrapped up tightly and numbed with anaesthetic, and he skated back onto the ice, where—in sudden-death overtime—he scored the winning goal. Unfortunately, in the excitement, Bobby forgot about his injury and began jumping up and down, yelling "Yahoo!" Ouch. Later, after drinking champagne from the Cup, Bobby finally got around to having an x-ray taken of his leg. It confirmed what everyone already knew: a fractured fibula.

Better than Huggies

In *Stanley Cup Fever*, Brian Macfarlane relates the following anecdote. After a Stanley Cup win in the 1960s, a press photo was taken with the bare-bummed three-month-old baby son of player Red Kelly sitting in the Cup. The baby gave a broad strained grin and, you guessed it, pooped in Stanley. It was, in Kelly's words, "a big dump right in the cup." Remembering his son's contribution to Stanley's trophy, Red Kelly says, "I think of that every time I see players drinking out of that bowl each spring."

A Chip Off the Old Block

And speaking of children, Brian McFarlane adds this tale to Stanley lore as well. Coach Scotty Bowman named his son Stan in honor of the Cup and, as a nickname, began calling the kid "Stanley Cup." Over time, the boy began to believe that this was in fact his full name. He discovered the truth only after his father registered him at school under the name Stanley Glenn Bowman. The poor little guy cried all the way home. "You mean my name really isn't Stanley Cup?" he said between sobs. To which his dad replied, in one of those touching father–son moments, "Stanley, you'll always be Stanley Cup to me." It makes one get all misty-eyed just thinking about it.

A Crime of Passion

In 1962, Stanley was almost stolen, but it was more a crime of passion than anything else. A diehard Montreal hockey fan was in Chicago, watching a playoff game. His beloved Canadiens were facing imminent elimination, and the fan could take it no more. He got up, walked to the lobby, where the Stanley Cup was on display, and smashed the glass. He then snatched up the Cup and made a break for the door. He was tackled and taken into court the following day. In his defense, he argued that he wasn't really stealing the Stanley Cup, he was merely returning it to where it belonged—Montreal. (Another version of this story has it happening in the 1961 in a game between Detroit and Chicago.)

Another Toronto Aberration

You may have noticed that the Toronto Maple Leafs have enshrined a misspelling in their very name (i.e., it should be the Maple Leaves; see Chapter 12 for the explanation) but what is less well known is that they have been misspelled by engravers as well. In one extended vowel-movement, the 1963 Stanley Cup champion Leafs appear on the Stanley Cup as "the *Leaes*." Sounds Hawaiian, don't you think? (The 1981 Islanders appear as "Ilanders.")

Stanley—Exposed!

In the 1980s, back when the Edmonton Oilers were still winning hockey games, a team tradition allowed each member of the team to keep the Cup for one day. Some of the more kindly players took it to children's hospitals and charity events, others took it home to meet the folks, but others—led by the irrepressible Mark Messier—escorted Lord Stanley's Cup on an all-night pub crawl that culminated with the Cup up on stage at a strip club while the girls danced about, peeling to the music and apparently incorporating Stanley into the act. (How, I'm not sure.)

When Stanley returned from one such engagement with a sizeable dent in his side ("Man, what a party!"), the more exuberant aspects of the Oiler tradition came to an end. And how did the Oilers repair Stanley's silver chalice? Did they take it to an accredited metalsmith? No. They took it to an auto repair shop where, no doubt, some greasy-handed mechanic named Louie said, "Yeah, sure. I can ding 'er back into shape." Men.

Will the Real Stanley Please Stand Up?

In 1991, a member of the Pittsburgh Penguins dove into Mario Lemieux's swimming pool with the Stanley Cup in his arms. It slipped away and ended up at the bottom. Or at least, that was one version of the story. In fact, the player *tossed* the Cup into the pool from the roof, narrowly missing the cement patio on the way. Rough-house like this may seem hard on a Victoria-era antique, but the truth is that since 1967 it is a stronger, sterling sliver replica that sits atop the trophy handed out and tossed around after each final. The original, frail silver-and-gold Cup is safe and sound and on display in a vault at the Hockey Hall of Fame in downtown Toronto. Or is it?

The switch between the real Cup and the sterling silver replica was a closely guarded secret. According to William Houston in *Pride & Glory*, it wasn't until 1970 that the truth came out, and that was only after thieves stole the Stanley Cup and demanded a $100,000 ransom. The NHL refused to pay, so the kidnappers sent back one of Stanley's ears. (Kidding!) In fact, the NHL finally, publicly admitted that the trophy being awarded annually was not in fact Lord Stanley's original rose bowl. The replica finally turned up in a Toronto parking lot and the case was never solved.

The current Stanley Cup, the one you see held aloft by victorious players, is also on display at the Hockey Hall of Fame. Unlike the antique original, this Stanley Cup is right out in the open, so you can touch it, fondle it, kiss it, and get your photo taken beside it. (Try not to get too carried away, however. It is a public place.)

In 1977, Stanley was almost stolen again, but an astute employee at the Hockey Hall of Fame noticed seven men with a large tool bag loitering nonchalantly around the Cup, and the jig was up.

Stanley x 3

It gets even more confusing. You may notice the Stanley Cup on proud display during CBC playoff broadcasts. It's a fake. Made o' plastic. Mere set decoration.

According to reporter Michael Ulmer, there are actually *three* Stanley Cups (not counting the CBC's piece of plastic): (1) the original silver bowl, (2) the Stanley Cup we see today, the one handed out, partied with, and filled with champagne, (3) a replica of the replica, a stand-in put on display when the "real replica" is on the road. Sound confusing? It is.

The Women in Stanley's Life

With the exception of Manon Rheaume (see Chapter 14), all of the players in the NHL have been men. It isn't just the players who have their names engraved on the Cup. Owners, coaches, and club presidents are also honored—there are more than 1,000 names engraved on Stanley. Among them are a handful of women:

- Marguerite Norris, president of the Detroit Red Wing Champions, was presented with the Stanley Cup in 1954 and 1955.
- Sonia Scurfield, co-owner of the Calgary Flames champions in 1989
- Marie Denise DeBartolo York, president of the Pittsburgh Penguins champions in 1991
- The Ilitch Clan. Mike Ilitch, owner of the Detroit Red Wings, made his wife and kids part-owners of the team, which assured that their names would be engraved on it when the Red Wings won in 1997 and again in 1998. It's a big family. Nine different Ilitches' names appear on Stanley, including Marian, Atanas, and Denise.

Ménage à Trois—Hockey Style

Talk about kinky. When Bryan Trottier of the New York Islanders had his "special time" with the trophy, he decided to take Stanley to bed. He asked his wife to make space—"just to see what it feels like. You know, just for one night, out of curiosity." Sure. That's what they all say.

Immaculate Conception: Stanley and the Miracle Birth

Cheryl Riley had been trying to get pregnant with her husband, Ken, for fifteen years. As a teenager, Cheryl had been told that a drug had accidentally rendered her infertile. She would never have children. The Rileys considered fertility drugs and *in vitro* fertilization and adoption. But in the end, all it took was the Stanley Cup and a magical kiss.

The story reads like a modern-day fairy tale, but it's true. Mike Ricci, a star player with the 1996 champions, the Colorado Avalanche, had a summer cabin near the Rileys' home. When Ricci invited people in the area to drop by to see the Cup, several hundred fans showed up, including Cheryl and Ken. Caught up in the spirit of the moment, Cheryl leaned over and gave the Stanley Cup a big wet kiss. That weekend, after seventeen years without birth control and countless attempts at getting pregnant, lightning struck. Cheryl was "With Child."

Nine months later, at the age of forty-two, Cheryl gave birth to a seven-pound baby boy. The doctors were mystified. Had Stanley played a miraculous role in these events? Was it reincarnation? Karma? Was it the ghost of Bill Barilko come back to earth? Or maybe Tim Horton, the player and donut czar who died tragically in a car crash? Cheryl laughs, but she won't rule it out. As Michael Ulmer noted in his report about these magical events: "Who knows? Maybe a hockey player's soul was looking for a home and it took the touch of the Stanley Cup to get him here."

And what did they name their son? Why, Stanley, of course. Stanley C. Riley. The middle initial stands for "Cup."

Diamonds Are a Team's Best Friend

When the Edmonton Oilers won their first Stanley Cup championship, the owner, a one-time used-car dealer from Ontario named Peter Pocklington, was feeling magnanimous. "Diamond rings for everyone!" Peter was a notorious cheapskate, so the offer came as an unexpected and pleasant surprise. What the players soon discovered, however, was that Peter had chosen the size of the diamonds according to the perceived "worth" of the people involved. Wayne Gretzky received a huge rock, the equipment men received tiny, minuscule flecks of diamond.

It got even worse. When one of the coaching assistants took his diamond in to be appraised, it turned out to be a fake. The trainers had all been given fake diamonds. Wayne Gretzky, exhibiting far more class than Pocklington, quietly had the fake diamonds replaced at his own cost. Which raises a question: If Pocklington was handing out fake diamonds anyway, why didn't he go all out and make them *really big* fake diamonds?

A XXX Insult

True, Stanley has been bruised, dented, stolen, and invoked as an excuse by mobs of angry and/or joyous Montrealers. But the most flagrant insult to Stanley's pride, in terms of pure gall if nothing else, was perpetuated by—who else?—Peter "The Puck Stops Here" Pocklington. As owner of the champion Edmonton Oilers, Peter had his father's name surreptitiously engraved on the Cup, above the players' names. The League was not amused, and today you can still see the suture line of Xs that were used to cross it out. You really have to wonder about a man who thinks he can sneak a name like "Basil Pocklington" onto a national sports trophy without anyone noticing. I mean, that would be as crazy as trading Wayne Gretzky.

And Speaking of Wayne Gretzky ...

The Great One has never forgotten what the game is all about. Wayne Gretzky may have gone "Hockeywood," but he is still a kid at heart, and above all he yearns to hold aloft the Stanley Cup—just one more time. Right side up or upside down, it is still the central symbol of professional hockey.

"You know," says Gretzky in his autobiography, "I've held women and babies and jewels and money, but nothing will ever feel as good as holding that Cup." I bet Mr. Gretzky was sleeping on the couch for a while after Mrs. Gretzky read that book.

Light as a Feather

From its original height of 7 ½ inches, the Stanley Cup has grown, and now stands 3 feet tall and weighs 32 pounds. But that is not how the players, the fans, and the owners see it. It far outweighs anything else in their lives. And yet, it is as light as a feather when you finally win it. Back in 1920, the *Ottawa Citizen* described the Stanley Cup as "the celebrated piece of silverware which has caused so much strife, so much heartbreaking excitement and so much joy." If anything, the excitement, the joy, and the heartbreak have only gotten stronger.

When veteran hockey player Lanny McDonald finally won the Stanley Cup, reporters asked him how it felt to hold it. Did it weigh a lot? He smiled and replied, "There's no weight to it ... A guy could carry it forever."

The Conquering Warrior

The image of the hockey player hoisting the Cup above his head and holding it high to the roar of the crowds strikes a certain animalistic chord. In *The Stanley Cup*, sportswriter D'Arcy Jenish traces this ritual back to a spontaneous, sudden gesture by a specific player: Terrible Ted Lindsay in 1950. Describing the Cup as "a hallowed object, a gleaming icon," Jenish calls Lindsay's overhead heave of the Cup "a powerful new symbol of victory that would capture the imagination of the post-war, baby-boom generation."

This simple act of a player holding the Cup above his head was described by Jenish as follows:

> This gesture is ancient in origin and primitive in nature. Every player who holds the Cup above his head is responding to the same impulse that has seized the conquering warrior from time immemorial. It is the urge to stand on the hilltop or the rooftop to trumpet victory and show tangible proof of triumph.

Gosh. And you thought it was just a trophy.

Stanley: From '69 to '99

Let's be brutally honest here. Do you really care that the Quebec Bulldogs won the Stanley Cup in 1912? Or that the Detroit Red Wings won in 1943? Of course not. If you want to see a list of every single winner from 1893 on, there are all kinds of books, magazines, and sports encyclopedias available. Here in *The Girlfriend's Guide to Hockey*, we aren't as obsessed with dates and numbers. Instead of compiling a complete rundown, I decided just to list the last thirty years. Why '69 and '99? No reason, really, except that those two are favorites of mine:

Stanley: from '69 to '99

Year	Team	Year	Team
1969	Montreal Canadiens	1984	Edmonton Oilers
1970	Boston Bruins	1985	Edmonton Oilers
1971	Montreal Canadiens	1986	Montreal Canadiens
1972	Boston Bruins	1987	Edmonton Oilers
1973	Montreal Canadians	1988	Edmonton Oilers
1974	Philadelphia Flyers	1989	Calgary Flames
1975	Philadelphia Flyers	1990	Edmonton Oilers
1976	Montreal Canadiens	1991	Pittsburgh Penguins
1977	Montreal Canadiens	1992	Pittsburgh Penguins
1978	Montreal Canadiens	1993	Montreal Canadiens
1979	Montreal Canadiens	1994	New York Rangers
1980	New York Islanders	1995	New Jersey Devils
1981	New York Islanders	1996	Colorado Avalanche
1982	New York Islanders	1997	Detroit Red Wings
1983	New York Islanders	1998	Detroit Red Wings
		1999	Dallas Stars

Why are They Throwing Octopuses?

Strange Rituals and Odd Superstitions

Hockey is a very strange sport, with many bizarre superstitions and rituals. Your hockey guy may have a few quirks and odd habits around playoff time, maybe he doesn't shave or he wears his team jersey to bed, but this is pretty normal. What the professional hockey boys do for good luck is far from normal.

Good-Luck Fashion Sense

We know that even our hockey guys have lucky articles of clothing. There are the old t-shirts that are so thin you can read the newspaper through them. But if you even suggest that maybe its time for the "Canadiens Win the Cup 1986" to retire, your guy immediately pulls it on (so worn-out you can count his chest hairs through it) and tells you it's a fine shirt so don't touch it. I don't even want to think of all the "lucky" underwear out there that is so holey that you could drain spaghetti through it. If our guys are this bad, just imagine what happens to hockey players when millions of dollars depend on their luck and performance.

These boys are a little obsessive. It's a common ritual for players to put on their equipment in a certain order every time they dress. Some players dress right first: right sock first, then right skate. Other players dress left. Some players are superstitious about their equipment, like former NHL star Butch Goring, who wore the same beat-up old helmet that he had used since the minors. Chris Chelios won't put his game jersey on until all of his teammates have theirs on. Darryl Sittler has a lucky suit and tie that he credits for a record-breaking ten points in one game (six goals and four assists) and a five-goal game. He credits the lucky tie with an overtime goal in the Canada Cup. You don't want to know what happens if he wears his lucky underwear.

The Shave

This is a very disturbing ritual of hockey players. It's a initiation rite that involves tricking the chosen player into entering a room, tying him down, and shaving his body ... his whole body. There are many horrific stories about this ceremony, but all involve grown men being dry-shaved. I don't think you want to know any more than that.

Freaky Phil

Phil Esposito had many "quirky" superstitions. He would have teammates fix his shoulder pads and suspenders just right. He also had to wear something black under his Boston Bruins jersey (sometimes it was a t-shirt or a dickie). He had put on a black dickie for one game against the Toronto Maple Leafs, to pamper a cold, and scored three goals that game. He also dresses right to left.

Wacky Wayne's Trousers

You've seen it. It even became a fad among young boys. Wayne Gretzky tucks one side of his jersey into his pants, he even has a piece of Velcro sewn on to keep it in place. Does he do it to get that "I've just had my hand down my pants" look? No, it's a superstition and he maintains it for good luck. When he was a wee little Wayne, his jersey was too big so he had to tuck part of it in.

Hockey teams also have some very peculiar rituals and superstitions. A common one is to whack the goalie's pads as you enter the ice; others are far stranger and more disgusting.

Eat Your Vegetables

A WHA (now disbanded) team called the Ottawa Nationals had a nutritious good-luck charm. It was a half-eaten cob of corn that the team trainer had found abandoned outside the team's dressing room. The trainer picked up the cob and tossed it to Gavin Kirk, telling him that he got it from an old Indian. That night the Nationals won, and Kirk kept the corn cob. The team won the next three games. This was their longest winning streak that season, and everyone credited the cob. Soon it became part of the pre-game ceremony in their dressing room. Before going on the ice, Kirk would remove the cob from his glove, let six players rub it for luck, then pry out one kernel of corn and throw it at Ken Stephenson. The whole team would yell like crazed maniacs and then enter the ice. The Ottawa Nationals eventually went bankrupt.

Flying Octopuses

This is a well-known weird ritual. Detroit Red Wings fans throw slimy, smelly, ugly octopuses on the ice during the game for good luck. The fans do this so often that now the referees now threaten a two-minute delay-of-game penalty against Detroit if an octopus hits the ice. How did this icky ritual start? We can trace it back to one man, Jerry Cusimano.

Jerry's father was in the fish and poultry business, and after helping their dad, Jerry and his brother Pete often went to Red Wings games. It was April 1952 when this brilliant and disgusting idea struck. Detroit was in the Stanley Cup playoffs and they had won the last seven games in a row. They needed to win the next game to complete an unstoppable eight-game winning streak and get the Stanley Cup. Jerry came up with a good-luck charm for Detroit. He thought an octopus would be lucky because it had eight legs, symbolizing the eight games needed to win the Cup. So, on April 15, 1952, Jerry Cusimano pitched the first flying octopus onto the Detroit Olympia's ice. Apparently the octopus did the trick, the Red Wings beat the Canadiens 3-0 and won the Stanley Cup. Tragically Jerry was killed in a car accident shortly after he hurled his first octopus, but his brother Pete kept the tradition alive and was there to throw seafood when the team needed him.

Superstition Becomes Suspension

It happened in the spring of 1987, during the Stanley Cup playoffs. The Montreal Canadiens were playing the Philadelphia Flyers in the sixth game of the series. The start of the game was delayed fifteen minutes due to a bench-clearing brawl.

The Montreal Canadiens had developed a ritual where they would shoot the puck into the opponent's net after the pre-game warmup. It wasn't a big deal, and most people didn't even notice. But this night someone did. When Shane Corson and Claude Lemieux shot the puck into the net, after everyone had cleared the ice, Ed Hospodar (of the Flyers) took notice and offense. He was pissed that Montreal had invaded the Flyers' end, even during the warmups, and he attacked Lemieux. That was it. Both teams jumped back on the ice, and a major brouhaha ensued. All of this happened before the game officially started. When the fight finally ended, the two teams were fined more than $24,000 each, and Ed Hospodar was suspended for the rest of the playoffs.

All of this because of a silly superstition.

Hockey fans also have some outlandish and kinky rituals of their own. These activities usually involve throwing various objects, or themselves, on the ice or at the players and officials.

- **Chickens Can Fly**: At the Los Angeles Forum, a fan threw a live chicken dressed in the Kings' team colors, purple and gold, onto the ice from the stands.
- **Three Little Piggies**: In Quebec City, three small, terrified, and squealing pigs were let loose on the ice.
- **Incoming Gophers:** The University of Minnesota's hockey team is called the Golden Gophers. On road trips to the University of North Dakota, the Dakota fans would throw dead gophers on the ice. It's a good thing they weren't called the Minnesota Midgets.
- **Nutty Nudies**: One night in Maple Leaf Gardens a naked man jumped the boards and made a run for the Leafs' bench. He didn't make it. Another night, in the Los Angeles Forum, three women, described as "curvaceous," strutted from goal line to goal line in the buff. Now, goal line to goal line is a long way, 178 feet to be exact. How long do you think it would take you to walk 178 feet on ice in your bare feet? Granted, you would be hurrying because of the cold, but you would also be slipping and falling. So, my question is this: Why weren't they removed? I'd also like to know what the officials were "pretending" to do during this parade. I'm sure Don Cherry has a highlight of this "March of the Hockey Maidens" in one of his videos.

- **It's Raining Rubbers**: Not those kind of rubbers, the kind that slip over your shoes to protect against water damage. In the past, at the Montreal Forum it was customary to celebrate a goal by throwing your shoe rubbers on the ice.
- **Pennies from Heaven**: During the early part of the century, the towns of Northern Ontario were filled with rich mining moguls. Hockey players were paid very well to come and play in this area, often being given fat bonuses if they scored the winning goal. Large sums of money were bet on these games.

  After one particularly exciting game in Haileybury, Ontario, rich fans showered the ice with money. Players grabbed fluttering bills and pocketed dropping coins. Hefty goalie Bill Nicholson grabbed an old washtub, filled it with loot, and then turned it over, plunking his 300-pound body on top to guard his booty.

Official Chuckers

Fans are not the only ones getting rowdy and throwing things. Let's not forget the players themselves and the officials. One ref used to hurl his bell at especially annoying fans, and once, televised live in Boston, players charged into the stands, hunted down a fan who had been bothering them and began beating the man with his own shoe.

The Strangest Thing on Ice

Perhaps the strangest thing on ice (or at least the yuckiest) was Ivan Matulik's nose.

At the time of the accident, Ivan was playing for the Halifax Citadels of the American Hockey League. During the play, Ivan had collided with an opposing player whose skate had arced past his face, neatly slicing off the tip of his nose. By the time that everyone realized what had happened, the Zamboni had already passed over the ice. If there was any hope of reattaching Ivan to his schnoz tip, then the Zamboni's slush pile had to be sifted through. Sure enough, his nose was there, and since it had been on ice it was successfully reunited with the rest of Ivan's face.

A Family Ritual

The Sutter family, of Viking, Alberta, has a great hockey family ritual. Their tradition is to become NHL players, six out of the seven brothers are (Darryl, Brent, Duane, Brian, and the twins Rich and Ron). The seventh brother, Gary, almost made it.

The only hockey tradition we had growing up in my family was for my dad to stay up late, yell at the refs, jumping on the couch and keeping me awake. My personal ritual during this time was to bury my head in the pillow and plan his early entry into the old folks' home. A really mean old folks' home, the kind where, if I paid extra, they would feed my dad puréed Brussels sprouts exclusively and force him to watch "Barney" on TV.

Bruce:
Here is my own heartwarming first hockey memory: It is winter 1970. Over the next ten years the Canadiens de Montreal will win the Coupe Stanley six (!) times. I am three years old. It is Saturday night, and all across the country Canadian families are huddled around the TV, humming along to our country's second national anthem. Duh–duh–duh–duh–duh! Duh–duh–duh–duh–duh! Duh–duh–duh–duh–duh-DUH! Da-da-da-da-da-daaaaaa! My family settles in for the game in our home in the Montreal suburb of Roxboro.

On one side of the room sit my mother, my brother, and my sister. I sit on the other side, with my father. My dad grew up in Port Morien, Cape Breton, listening to hockey games on CBC Radio. He was and is an unshakable Leafs fan. When he was a child in the forties the Leafs were a force to be reckoned with; they won the Cup five times in that decade. The last year that Toronto had that honor was 1967, the year that I was born. Rather than lament the fact that the Leafs not only won the Cup that year, but beat the Habs to do it, I choose to take personal pride in the fact that they haven't won it since.

> As we sat watching the game,
> someone observed that the Canadiens fans
> (Mom, Sis, and Bro) were visibly separate from the Leaf fan (Dad).
> Why, it was asked, was I sitting in the Toronto section? As a three-year-
> old I had never had to choose sides before. If I undergo psychotherapy, I
> expect to discover that this was a formative moment in my young life:
> The first time I had to place myself on one side of an issue. I looked from
> my father to the TV (Guy Lafleur in flight, an awe-inspiring image at any
> age), to the rest of my family eagerly entreating me to jump ship.
> And then ... I crossed the room. From that day forward,
> I was a Habs fan.
> Sorry, Dad.

Don't pity my father, though. Leafs fans thrive on adversity, they have no choice. Dad and I are still able to enjoy hockey together-in the mid-80s we had season tickets for the Fredericton Express. The Express were the AHL farm team of the now defunct Quebec Nordiques. Dad and I went to forty home games together. We cheered the wins, analyzed the losses, and ate the unspeakable hockey-game popcorn. This despite what appears to be the prevailing wisdom among concession holders: "Well, the watered down pop is disgusting. If we cake enough salt on the pop-corn, they'll have no choice but to drink it."

Magic Potions

A team will maintain any silly superstition and try any gimmick that may give them a winning edge.

Over the years, teams have tried some very strange things to improve their play. In the 1960s the Detroit Red Wings briefly kept a tank of oxy-gen at their bench to give players a boost. They also kept a container of yogurt in the dressing room, expecting players to gobble a spoonful each time they passed by, to improve their performance.

The New York Rangers also were known for their gimmicks. The coach once had each team member drink a glass of hot water in the morn-ing to get them going. He also subjected them to a "Magic Elixir" created by a famous New York restaurateur from a recipe by Momma Leone. They once went so far as to have their players hypnotized, but found them to be too sluggish and had to call it off.

As you can see, hockey is full of weirdos: playing and watching. But I guess I didn't have to tell you that—you're sleeping with one.

Who is the Man Behind the Mask?

Goalies and Other Wildlife

Here's your job description: You will be put in front of a net, people will hurl themselves and a frozen, rock-hard, chunk of rubber at you at speeds exceeding 90 miles per hour. This will happen sixty or seventy times in a span of one hour and you must stop everything coming your way, with no regard for your personal safety. If you mess up (allowing anything to pass by you), a red light will go off and thousands of people will curse you. The pay for this job is very good, but you will probably have a nervous breakdown. Interested?

A goalie's job is very tough. He must be part of the action but still remain slightly removed from it and ahead of it. He is the only player on the ice who can see the full game. He must feel the patterns of the plays and adapt to them. Even if a team is having a bad night, if the goalie is "on," the game can be saved. The goalie is under a lot of pressure to perform at his peak every game, every night.

It is for these reasons that goalies are generally the most "eccentric" players in hockey. They have a kind of mystic place on the team, and their teammates go out of their way to protect them. Pity the player who goes in on a goalie or makes the mistake of shoving or hitting him. He will face the wrath of the assaulted goalie's entire team. Even if a player bumps or gets too close to the goalie, there will be repercussions. However, if a goalie comes out of the net for a little naughtiness of his own, and the attacked player retaliates, that player is *still* in for trouble from the goalie's friends. When a goalie gets caught being a bad boy, he does not serve his own penalty, one of his teammates does.

A goalie does most of his work in his crease. The crease is a sacred space; if there is an opposing player in it (obstructing the goalie), then the goal is disallowed. The goalie often comes out of the crease to cut down the angle of shots or to direct the puck to his defensemen. Mind you, the goalie is restricted to his half of the ice and cannot cross the center red line.

The goalie's training is slightly different from that of other players. He often has his own trainer and focuses more on agility and reflexes than on speed and stamina.

Throughout hockey history, there have been many amazing goalies. Here are a few of the most famous, the top dogs, the big kahunas.

Georges Vezina

Georges Vezina was known for his cool presence on the ice. He played with a calm dignity and a poker face, and for these reasons he was named the "Chicoutimi Cucumber" (after his home town). He played for fifteen years with Montreal, from 1910 to 1925.

Montreal discovered Vezina when they were doing an exhibition tour of Quebec in February 1910. A game had been arranged between the powerful pros and the Chicoutimi amateurs. Vezina surprised Montreal when he, an amateur, shut out the king Canadiens. Montreal promptly signed him, and in the fall of that same year he was playing for them. With Vezina's help, the Montreal Canadiens won two Stanley Cups.

Vezina was a quiet man who never complained. His life revolved around his family: his wife and his twenty-two children. Yup, twenty-two.

On November 28, 1925, Montreal was playing Pittsburgh. After a scoreless first period, Vezina left the ice, bleeding from the mouth. He collapsed in the dressing room, but returned to the ice, only to collapse again. Vezina left the ice for the last time, and only then did his family and friends learn that he had tuberculosis. Four months later, at the age of thirty-nine, he died.

In memory of the quiet and dignified goalie, the Vezina Trophy was born. The trophy is give out to the NHL's top goalie each year.

Terry Sawchuck

It's amazing that Terry Sawchuck survived such a long career, twenty-one years, from 1949 to 1970, all during days when goalies didn't wear

slew foot

Shinny

crease

Blades

Grinder

masks. This poor man had a long list of injuries, including a broken right arm that never healed properly and ended up inches shorter than the other; severed tendons in his hand; a fractured instep; a punctured lung; ruptured discs; bone chips in his elbows that required three operations; a ruptured appendix; and innumerable cuts on his face and body, one of which almost cost him the sight in his right eye.

Terry became a goaltender in a very sad way. When Terry was ten years old, his brother, who was a goalie, developed a heart murmur and died. Terry inherited his goalie equipment and began to play. Seven years later, he broke into hockey with Omaha of the U.S. Hockey League. Throughout his long career he played for Detroit (several times), Boston, Toronto, Los Angeles, and the New York Rangers. He won the Vezina three times and shared a fourth. Sawchuck ended his career in New York in 1970 and, shortly after his last game, died of a pulmonary embolism. He was the only goalie ever to record more than 100 career shutouts.

Glen Hall

Glen Hall was the iron man of hockey. He played 552 consecutive games (including playoff games) in an era when goalies didn't wear masks, and—as might be expected—he suffered many cuts and concussions. His playing streak ended only when he allowed a goal because of a back injury so severe he couldn't bend over to stop the puck.

Hall first played for the Detroit Red Wings in the 1955–56 season, before moving on to the Chicago Blackhawks. He played ten years with Chicago, winning three Vezinas and helping Chicago win their first Stanley Cup in twenty-three years. Hall also introduced the popular "butterfly stance" for goaltenders. Rather than keeping arms and legs close together, the butterfly stance opens up a little more, thus allowing the goalie to cover more of the net.

I think secretly Glen Hall didn't want to be a goalie. At the end of each season he would notify the Blackhawks organization that he was considering retiring. Each year Chicago would come back with a fat and juicy contract, luring Hall to stay. When the new season began Hall would always doubt his choice. In the 1967 expansion draft, St. Louis plucked Hall from Chicago's roster. This time Hall was really going to quit hockey. At the age of thirty-six, he wanted to return to his true love— the Alberta soil. He owned an 160-acre farm in Alberta and wanted to retire and be a farmer. St. Louis offered Hall the biggest salary ever at that time ($45,000), and Hall packed away his overalls and hoe. He played for St. Louis and, in the 1968–69 season, he shared the Vezina with Jacques Plante. He finally retired at the end of the 1970–71 season.

Ken Dryden

Ken Dryden was famous for his "Thinker" stance in goal. When the play had stopped, Dryden would prop himself up, leaning his gloves on the end of his stick, and drop his chin onto his gloves. It was so cute, like a puppy posing for a pat on the head. When the play resumed, Dryden was no puppy, he was a giant brick wall. At 6'4", 205 pounds, he filled the net.

During his relatively short career, 1971–79, Dryden won or shared five Vezinas and helped the Montreal Canadiens win six Stanley Cups (four in succession).

Dryden was famous not only for his amazing goalie talents, but also for his intellect. Ken Dryden was hockey's scholar-athlete. He worked his way through Cornell University and law school on money earned through his hockey talents. He took a sabbatical from the Canadiens during the 1973–74 season to fulfill his law-school requirements by working in a Toronto law firm for $137 a week.

Ken Dryden was a rarity in hockey: the game needed him more than he needed to play. When he retired in 1979, members of the hockey world were surprised. He was thirty-one, at the peak of his career, and was earning $200,000 a year. Everyone thought he was retiring to pursue a law career or move into politics, but Dryden surprised them again. He and his family, wife and two children, moved to England, where he wrote a book on his hockey experiences. Today, Dryden is still involved in the game: he is the president of the Toronto Maple Leafs.

The list of great goalies could go on and on, including such old-time stopping wonders as Turk Broda, Frankie Brimsek, Bill Durnan, and Gump Worsley. The top goalies of today to watch are Patrick Roy of Colorado, Curtis Joseph of Toronto, Chris Osgood of Detroit and the unbeatable Dominik "The Dominator" Hasek of Buffalo.

Goalie Protection

Goalies are the most padded player on the team. They have to be, to be protected from speeding pucks, overactive sticks, and player collisions. Their equipment has evolved from its frighteningly sparse beginnings, when netminders strapped their skate blades on to their boots, shoved magazines in their pants to protect their, um, shins, and played barefaced. Bobby Hull, whose slapshot would one day be clocked at 118 miles (190 km) an hour, began playing during the maskless era. Think about the kind of people willing to throw their face in front of that.

As the game has changed, goalie equipment has been adapted. When curved hockey sticks became popular and shots on goal harder and higher, goalies began to wear more padding and—finally—masks. The evolution of goalie pads, pants, and gloves took place in the first half of the 1900s, but it wasn't until the 1970s that these guys finally clued in and started wearing masks regularly.

The first goalie mask actually appeared in 1898, when a goalie donned a crude iron mask and was promptly jeered and booed by his fans. Clint Benedict wore a primitive leather mask in 1929 to protect a broken nose, but only for a game or two. After his nose healed, off went the mask.

The NHL goalie famous for the first use of a mask is Jacques Plante, then of the Montreal Canadiens. Plante had devised a facemask to wear during practices to protect a fractured cheekbone and facial cuts he'd received. But on November 1, 1959, Plante had to wear his mask during a regular game against the New York Rangers. Plante had tripped Ranger Andy Bathgate. Bathgate retaliated by deliberately shooting the puck at Plante's face. Plante had to leave the ice. He returned with stitches and a cream-colored plastic facemask. Montreal won the game and began an eighteen-game winning streak. The mask seemed to give Plante a new confidence, and soon other goalies started to wear masks. Plante continued to modify the goalie's mask, and he had a hand in the design of every mask during his time.

Painting the goalie's mask became trendy in the ever tasteful 1970s. Gilles Gratton had a ferocious tiger's head on his mask, Garry Edwards had a cobra, and Gerry Cheevers painted marks on his mask to look like the stitches he would have received had he not been protected by fiberglass. But I think Gaye Cooley missed the point of painting your mask when he had a big Happy Face painted on the front of his. A yellow grinning goof is not intimidating!

Hit in the Head Too Many Times: Goalie Stories

The Oldest Excuse

Gilles "the Cat" Gratton was one of the first goalies to wear a painted facemask in the 1970s. He wore a tiger-striped visor while playing for the New York Rangers. Gilles acquired his nickname when he claimed to have past lives, not nine but hundreds. Gilles believed in the reincarnation of souls; in fact, he used his past lives as an excuse not to play hockey. He once told his coach, John Ferguson, that he couldn't play one night because he had injured his leg. When the coach asked him how he'd hurt it, he replied, "I was a soldier in the Franco-Prussian War of 1870 and was wounded in the leg. It still bothers me from time to time." Gratton was completely serious. And a year later, he was completely unemployed.

Goalie as a Team Captain

Bill Durnan was the last goalie to serve as a team captain. His many trips out of the net to bring issues to the referee prompted the league to change the rule allowing the goalie to act as captain.

Knitting Needles and Goalie Sticks

Goalie great Jacques Plante, whose career spanned twenty years, was not a social man. He didn't form close friendships with his teammates, and when his team was on the road, instead of going out with the boys for a night of rowdy, raunchy fun, Jacques would stay in his room, knitting toques and reading fan mail.

Shutout Kings

Alex Connell of the Ottawa Senators set the NHL record for most consecutive shutouts. In the 1927–28 season, he played a six-game streak: that is 461 minutes and 29 seconds without allowing a goal. The record still stands today.

But Terry Sawchuck holds the record for most career shutouts. A record 103 in his twenty-season career.

Goalie Striptease

Gary Smith was a very nervous goalie. To relieve tension and get his mind off the game, he would perform a "goalie's striptease" between periods. At the end of each period, Smith would take off all of his equipment and then promptly put it back on again. This is a long process when you're wearing 30 pounds of equipment. It would have been less tiring for him if he had just learned zen meditation.

Big, Bad Barfer

Glen Hall's nerves were even worse than Smith's. Hall, who played eighteen seasons, threw up before every game, and often between periods. Here's a guy who probably didn't have many lockerroom buddies.

"Hall, don't sit beside me."

"Aw, come on. I feel fine."

"You sure?"

"Yeah, I'm feeling good, steady as a rock."

"You look green, you want some Gravol or a little ginger root to chew?"

"Really, I'm okay."

"All right, you can sit here. Wait, Hall, you are lookin' really green ... Move! ... Get outta here! ... Aww, man, Hall got me again. Anybody got a clean jersey?"

You can understand the dilemma, Hall was an amazing goalie, but he was also an amazing barfer. Everyone admired Glen Hall (from a distance).

Super Goalie

George Hainsworth, of the Montreal Canadiens, recorded twenty-two shutouts in the forty-four game season of 1928–29. He allowed only forty-three goals that year. No goalie since has come close to that record.

Five on One

Coach Eddie Shore had a temper. One time when he didn't agree with a ref's call, he pulled his whole team from the ice. Unfortunately, the team's goalie, Don Simmons, was busy cleaning his crease and didn't hear Shore's call. The referee warned Shore that if he didn't return the rest of his team to the ice pronto, the game would go on without them. Shore crossed his arms and turned away like a sulking two-year-old. The ref took one look at the stubborn coach and dropped the puck. The game resumed without Shore's players, except the goalie. Simmons finally looked up when the puck dropped, only to see five players skating full speed at him. He panicked as the skaters passed the puck, pinballing it at light speed from one to another. He blocked the first shot, then another; two more followed and he successfully redirected them. The last shot missed the net but flew back through the edge of the crease. Simmons dove onto the puck, holding it long enough to draw a whistle and get the rest of his team on the ice. Don Simmons survived the first—and so far the only—five on one in hockey history.

Scoring Goalies

I bet you didn't know goalies could score. It's happened not once, but an incredible three times in NHL history.

Billy Smith of the New York Islanders was the first goalie credited with a goal. Smith didn't actually shoot the puck in; he just happened to be the last player to touch the puck before an opposing player shot it into his own net.

Ron Hextall of the Philadelphia Flyers was the first goalie to shoot the puck and score. He did it twice, both empty-net goals, once on the Boston Bruins in 1988 and later that season in the playoffs against the Washington Capitals.

The third netminder to score was Martin Brodeur of the New Jersey Devils. Brodeur scored an empty-net goal against the Montreal Canadiens in the 1997 playoffs. I am proud to say I witnessed this historical hockey moment. Bruce and I were watching the game when Brodeur took the shot. The puck crossed the red line, almost in slow motion, and continued into Montreal's zone. We held our breath as it headed for Montreal's crease and into the net. It was magical. Even though Bruce is a diehard I-don't-care-what-anyone-says-they'll-win-the-Cup Canadiens fan, he was amazed. The next day I watched a television interview with Brodeur. He was very cool about it, acting very professional, but I could tell that it was all he could do to not jump up on the interviewer's desk and do an "I'm so cool" dance.

Here's a bit of trivia to stump your guy. These three goalies are not the only ones credited with a goal. Early goalies were expected to stay on

The Crease

Glove Hand

Wristshot

Left Wing Lock

their feet during the entire game, but they were free to play the whole ice (originally they were not restricted to their side of the red center line). Goalies could leave their net to race up the ice to try to score, but few ever did. In 1905, Montreal goalie Fred Brophy took the chance and flew up the ice to score. Late in the 1906, season Brophy pulled the same trick to score again.

Biggest Bad-Boy Goalie

Billy Smith was one of hockey's nastiest goalies. He played eighteen seasons, from 1971 to 1989, for Los Angeles and then the New York Islanders. He was known for giving chopping blows to the legs and spears to the groin, delivered from his net. He was also famous for his "Ted Bundy Sleeper" move, where he'd slither out of his cage and knock out players with a lethal blow from his blocker to the back of the head. This was a guy you didn't want to mess with!

Fans Play Keep-Away

During the 1971 Stanley Cup playoffs, as the Toronto Maple Leafs faced the New York Rangers, the New York fans were feeling playful. During the game, Vic Hadfield, of New York, skated in on Toronto's goalie, Bernie Parent, and ripped his mask off his face. Parent was furious, and when he tried to grab it back, Hadfield threw it into the crowd of rowdy fans. Parent went to the sideboards, but the fans had already began a game of "Keep-Away" and the mask was lost high in the crowd. Parent was unable to play without his mask, so Toronto's backup goalie was called to the ice. Ironically, Toronto's backup was none other than Jacques Plante, the man famous for wearing hockey's first NHL goalie's mask.

Oh, Oh

Bernie Parent wore the numbers 00 on the back of his jersey when he played for the WHA. Why? Bernie explained to the media, "Every time a puck gets past me and I look back in my net, I say, 'Oh, oh.'"

Oh, Brother

We all know how competitive brothers can be within a family. Imagine how they are on ice.

When Tony Esposito made his NHL debut, he had to face his already-a-hockey-hero brother, Phil. Phil was playing his sixth season in the NHL and had been breaking scoring records when he faced his brother on December 5, 1968.

Both brothers were nervous before the game; Phil wanted his brother to do well, and Tony had to face not only a team that was tearing the league apart, but also his record-setting brother. The game began, and eight minutes into the first period, Phil Esposito scored on his little brother. He did it again in the third period, but the game ended in a 2-2 tie. It was poetic justice for both brothers.

Coach Saves the Day

It was the spring of 1928 when the coach of the New York Rangers, Lester Patrick, showed great courage (or complete lack of sanity) and saved the game. The Rangers were playing the Montreal Maroons during the Stanley Cup finals. They had lost the first game, and the second was a scoreless tie, when New York's goalie jumped to stop a goal and caught the puck over his left eye. He collapsed to the ice. These were the days before teams carried a backup goalie, and New York had no replacement for their downed netminder. In despair, Lester Patrick, then forty-four, with his hockey-playing days far behind him and having never played the goal position, suited up. Patrick made some great saves. With two minutes left, Montreal scored on him, and the game went into overtime. There were seven long, nail-biting minutes of overtime before New York's Frank Boncher scored on Montreal, ending Lester Patrick's goaltending days and winning the game.

Make Love, Not Goals

Who was hockey's only hippy?

Before playing for the Montreal Voyageurs, Ken Dryden spent the summer traveling from Luxembourg to Istanbul in a Volkswagen van with his wife. The happy hippies slept in a tent, cooked their own food, and spent an average of $10.17 a day.

A Goalie Couple

In 1904 the Ottawa Senators faced the Rat Portage Thistles in the Stanley Cup playoffs. It had been a hard, dirty series, full of tricks, butt-ends, cross-checks, and body slams. The frustrated, bruised, and bleeding Thistles decided to put two men in goal (apparently there were no limits on the number of goalies back then). They played that way for the entire game, making it twice as difficult for Ottawa to score. But Ottawa still won the game.

Hockey's Renaissance Man

King Clancy was hockey's renaissance man. He played every position, including goal. In the days where goalies would serve their own penalties, Clancy would take over for his netminder, Clint Benedict, when Benedict was being a bad boy.

Replay Oooops

John Garrett's face is probably still red. Garrett was the Hartford Whalers' starting goalie in a game against the Washington Capitals. He was fascinated by the huge replay screen in the Washington arena, a little too fascinated. When the Caps scored on him, he was sure that the puck had not quite crossed the goal line. Garrett decided to watch the replay to confirm his suspicions. Unfortunately, he was oblivious to the fact that the game had resumed. By the time that the distracted Garrett heard his teammates screaming, it was too late. The Capitals scored their second goal within a matter of seconds, and the Whalers' coach pulled Garrett from the net, replacing him with the backup goaltender. Garrett could now watch the replays uninterrupted for the rest of the game.

Nicknames

Each goalie has been crowned with a nickname. Some are very intimidating and some are downright goofy. Here are a few:

Nicknames That Work

    "Cujo"—Curtis Joseph
    "The Dominator"—Dominik Hasek
    "Godzilla"—Olaf Kolzig
    "Hail Cesare"—Cesare Maniago
    "Billy the Kid" or "The Axe"—Billy Smith
    "Whacker"—Darcy Wakaluk

Nicknames That Don't Quite Work

    "Poops"—Daren Puppa
    "Peanut Butter Boy"—Jeff Reese
    "Praying Bennie"—Clint Benedict
    "The Glasgow Gobbler"—Andy Aikenhead
    "Blind Blake"—Mike Blake
    "Giggles"—Jean-Sebastien Giguere
    "Sugar Jim"—Jim Henry
    "Trees"—Mark LaForest
    "Tubby"—Ken McAuley

Is Gretzky Really all That Great?

A Field Guide to Hockey Heroes

Wayne Gretzky is one player you rapidly become familiar with when you start to follow hockey. There's a lot of Gretzky talk out there. Lots of Gretzky adulation and a fair amount of Gretzky bashing. When he retired it was Wayne-O-Rama. Every TV station, radio program, magazine and newspaper mourned his departure. It was all Wayne, all the time.

So one day I turned to Bruce and asked, in all seriousness mind you:

"So, is Gretzky really that good?"

"Gretzky?" he said.

"Yes," I said.

"WAYNE Gretzky?" he said.

"Yes, yes, is he really that good?"

"So, you're asking me, is Wayne Gretzky really that good?" He looked at me now like I was exhibiting the classic symptoms of some kind of neural disorder.

"Yes."

"At hockey. Wayne Gretzky. Oilers. Stanley Cup. You're asking me if Wayne Gretzky is really that good at hockey, is that what you're asking me now?" He could hardly have been more surprised if I had asked "So, this breathing thing, we need to do it to live, huh?"

"Never mind." I said, "Just never mind."

I have since read Wayne Gretzky's autobiography and I have seen him play. Now I have a sense of how incomprehensible my question must have seemed at the time.

Who's the Best? Opinions Vary

Bruce, Will, and I sat down to sort out once and for all who the real top ten all-time players were. Unfortunately, our brainstorming session rapidly degenerated into name-calling and threatened "fisticuffs." Yet another lesson learned: hockey fans are eternally faithful to their favorite players and will defend them to the bitter (often *very* bitter) end.

We decided to retire to our respective corners and each produce a list. Bruce's is suspiciously heavy on Canadiens players, Will's is suspiciously lacking in the same. Mine is, of course, the definitive list, so we'll save that for last.

Rant on boys …

Bruce's All-Time Top Ten Players List

This carefully crafted list is the result of many hours of painstaking research and thoughtful deliberation. I have compared the statistics, records, speed, skill, IQ, fashion sense, and personal hygiene of NHL players past and present. These ten represent the *crème de la crème* of more than 100 years of professional hockey competitors.

Okay, maybe my selection process was a little less stringent. My choices are actually based, more or less equally, on career duration, points accumulated, contribution to the game, and, lastly, whether or not the player in question played for the Montreal Canadiens at any time. Try as I might, I could not pass over Gretzky, Lemieux, Howe, or Orr in favor of, say, Guy Carbonneau. Or Pete Mahovlich. Or his brother Frank. Phil Esposito. Jacques Lemaire. Serge Savard. Denis Savard. Bob Gainey …

1. Gretzky: The Great One

Gretzky started skating at age two, and he was setting records at age six. By the tender age of fifteen, when most adolescent boys are a gangling tangle of arms, legs, and embarrassment, Wayne Gretzky was a nationally known talent and the subject of a televised documentary. He entered the NHL in 1979, when the Edmonton Oilers, from the now defunct World Hockey Association (WHA), were adopted as an expansion team.

The Oilers, young, cocky, and brimming with talent, embarked on the journey that would lead them to four Stanley Cups in five years (1984–88). As the team improved and deepened, long-standing NHL records began to fall. Gretzky set new records for points, assists, and goals scored, only to break his own record the next season. Actually, it doesn't do Gretzky justice to say that he merely "broke" NHL records. He broke records in much the same sense that Godzilla broke Tokyo. We're

The Great One

talking chomping, stomping, fire-breathing destruction here. His All-Time Regular Season Assist record is 1,843. Paul Coffey is second, with 1,063. Gordie Howe holds second place in All-Time Regular Season Points, with 1,846; Gretzky's number one count is 2,705.

Gretzky is a humble and gracious ambassador for the game of hockey. This is attributed to his dad. Walter Gretzky made sure his son understood that his talent bestowed upon him a responsibility to give back as well as he received.

The Art Ross Trophy for regular-season scoring has gone to Gretzky ten times. He won the Hart Trophy, given for most points in regular-season play, every year from 1980 to 1989, skipping only 1988. That year the trophy went to Mario Lemieux.

2. Mario Lemieux: "The Best" One

By 1984 Pittsburgh fans, players, and owners had suffered through seventeen long years of losing seasons, low attendance, and even a team bankruptcy in 1975. And then …

"Unto us a player is born and he shall lead us from our torment and his name shall be Super Mario," I imagine the Pens faithful cried out as they prostrated themselves before their new Messiah. Well, okay, maybe not. But you have to understand the way hockey fans can act when they smell a chance at the Cup.

A Stanley Cup contender isn't built in a single season, however, especially when one guy is doing most of the work. From 1984 to 1990, Mario won the Lester B. Pearson Award (Outstanding Player) twice, the Hart Trophy (Team MVP) once, and the Art Ross Trophy (Regular-Season Scoring) twice. In the same period the Penguins made it to the playoffs … once.

In 1987, Lemieux played in the Canada Cup. He scored a tournament-high eleven goals, including the Cup winner against Russia in the third game in a best-of-three series.

If I may just wax poetic on that play for a moment:

A minute and twenty-six seconds left in the game, score tied at two. Two Team Canada players break out of their zone and streak down the ice. Who is it? It's Wayne Gretzky (gasp!) and … Mario Lemieux (gasp! gasp!) They fly in over the blue line. Gretzky drop pass to Lemieux (let us take a moment to revel in the glorious rapture of that phrase), Lemieux shoots … SCORES!! Canada up by a goal with a minute and change to go. Oh, the unbridled beauty of it all!

Okay, okay, so maybe it wasn't that important a moment globally speaking, but Lord, it was pretty. For a young Canadian male who was only five when the '72 series was played, I have to take my moments where I can find them.

But what of Mario? As the 1990s began, things got both better and worse. During the 1989–90 season he missed twenty-one games due to a herniated disk in his back. A spinal infection sidelined Lemieux for the first fifty games of the 1990–91 season. For the team, however, things were looking up. In 1991, the Penguins won their first Stanley Cup. The next year Mario was back full-time, and so was the magic. Pittsburgh racked up Cup number two. The following season brought more bad news for Lemieux. In January 1993, he announced that he had been diagnosed with Hodgkin's disease. Radiation treatments and recovery kept him out of the game until March.

A variety of afflictions, mainly affecting his back, forced Lemieux to miss sixty-two games during the 1993–94 season. He chose to sit out the entire 1994–95 season, shortened to only forty-eight games by a player lockout. He returned for the next two seasons, before announcing his retirement in 1997.

After undergoing the last of his radiation treatments on March 2, 1993, Lemieux flew to Philadelphia for a game against the Flyers. He picked up a goal and an assist. It is that kind of heart and dedication to the game that puts Lemieux head and shoulders above so many of the players in the NHL today.

3. Gordie Howe: Even Wayne Gretzky Has a Hero

A long, long time ago, before the era of Wayne Gretzky, fans and eager young players with NHL dreams had to look elsewhere for their heroes. This period is known in Edmonton as "S.B.G.," or "Sometime Before Gretzky." Little is known of hockey in Alberta's capital city before this time. Wayne Gretzky grew up, of course, at the close of the S.B.G. period. As young Wayne skated, shot, and passed his way ever closer to the dawn of a new age, it was Mr. Hockey, Gordie Howe, that he was trying to emulate.

Years later, when Gretzky began toppling NHL records, the numbers that he surpassed would be those of his hero. Gretzky confessed to having mixed feelings about breaking Howe's all-time points record.

Gordie Howe played much of his thirty-three years in professional hockey with the Detroit Red Wings. During that time he celebrated four

Stanley Cup wins and amassed 1,846 points. He ranked among the league's top five scorers for twenty years in a row.

When playing against Howe, being scored on was only one of your worries. Mr. Elbow, as he was sometimes called, adopted a skating style that brought his elbows up around his ears (and everyone else's) with each stride. Defending against Howe brought with it the very real risk of serious personal injury. And Heaven help you if you dared to drop the gloves with Gordie.

Despite his penchant for mixing it up on the ice, Howe was a family man. He even played professional hockey with his two sons, the only player ever to do so, when he was with the Houston Aeros of the WHA.

4. Bobby Orr: Hey, It's Bobby Orr

When I was a young lad growing up in a suburb of Montreal, my parents signed me up for hockey. I was Number 4 on a team called the Bruins. I played defense. It is here that any similarity between myself and Bobby Orr ceases. Bobby Orr played defense for the Boston Bruins and played it very, very well. If pressed for a reason as to why Orr is on this list, my immediate response would be "*Pfft*, hey, it's Bobby Orr." I realize, of course, that this does not technically constitute a reason, but you had to be there. Orr's stats are impressive: twelve years, two Stanley Cups, and 915 points. He was the first defenseman to ever win the NHL scoring title.

In 1966, Orr came to the Bruins in much the same way Mario Lemieux came to the Pens, straight from the draft and carrying the hopes of a near hopeless team on his shoulders. Boston hadn't broken 50 points on the season for six years. In 1967, they finished with 44. In 1968, their final tally was *84*. That figure rose to 100 points in 1969. The following year the Bruins won their first Stanley Cup since 1941.

The number of points that Orr scored are only half of the story of his impact on the game. On his way to the net, he challenged the tried-and-true rules for playing an attacker. His speed and agility left opposing players frozen in place. Once Orr took possession of the puck, the only way he wanted to give it up was by putting it in your net.

Recurring knee problems and the cumulative effect of surgery after surgery to correct them eventually forced Orr out of the game. Like Lemieux's, Orr's desire to play burned brightly, but his body could no longer stand the constant punishment.

5. Guy Lafleur: Don't Call Him "The Flower"

If I had a hockey hero as a kid, it was Lafleur. I had his picture on my wall and my prized Sher-Wood Guy Lafleur Official Hockey Stick. In his seventeen years in the NHL (fourteen with the Canadiens), he won five Stanley Cups (all with the Canadiens) and collected 1,353 points. He remains the last Canadien to win a scoring championship or a Hart Trophy.

Hockey broadcasters would occasionally call Guy Lafleur "The Flower." I hated it when they did that. It *is* a literal translation of his name, but *not* a stirring hockey image. Sometimes they would use the phrase "Flower Power," which was only marginally less uninspiring. It was the 1970s, and things were strange.

Most of Lafleur's playing days occurred in the time before helmets were mandatory, or even popular. The classic Lafleur image is of him streaking down the ice with his blond hair streaming out behind him, *le demon blond*.

Lafleur retired from professional hockey in 1985. He returned briefly with the New York Rangers in 1988 before moving on to the Canadiens' arch-nemesis, the Quebec Nordiques.

I remember the first game that he played in the Montreal Forum with Quebec. Habs fans gave him a warm welcome at the start of the game, no hard feelings. Indeed, if anyone should have carried a grudge it should have been Lafleur himself. When he announced his return to the NHL, the Montreal organization passed on him.

Early in the game, fans were treated to a glimpse into the past. Lafleur broke in on the Montreal netminder, unleashed a trademark blast from just inside the blue line, and scored. The Forum erupted, just like old times. Guy Lafleur had scored; it didn't matter whose sweater he was wearing.

6. Maurice "The Rocket" Richard: He Was a Riot

When Maurice Richard headed for the net, he took off in a straight line, like a rocket. He led Montreal to eight Stanley Cup victories over his eighteen years with the club. A career total 965 points included 50 goals in 50 games one season, an NHL first. He finished among the league's top five scorers fifteen times while playing for the Canadiens.

He was the player fans looked to for the big play when the Habs needed a boost. The playoffs were no exception: Richard holds the record for playoff winners in overtime (six goals) and shares the mark for most goals in a playoff game, at five.

In the deciding game of the semi-final series against Boston in 1952, Richard was knocked unconscious in a collision with an opposing player. After spending much of the game in the dressing room, he returned to the bench and asked for the score and the time remaining. He couldn't read the score clock himself; he still couldn't see that far. Half-conscious, he took to the ice, stripped the puck from a Bruins defender, and scored the winning goal.

In 1955, NHL president Clarence Campbell suspended Richard from the league for hitting a linesman. The response by Canadiens fans is now known as the "Rocket Richard Riot." Not that it's hard to get Montrealers to riot, mind you. Jubilant fans and opportunistic bystanders caused a post–Stanley Cup victory riot following the Canadiens' win in 1986. Several years later, disgruntled fans facing a Guns N' Roses/Metallica concert cancellation took to the streets as well.

Imagine getting that upset about a *concert*. I mean, it's not like it was hockey.

7. Henri Richard: The Pocket Rocket

What do you do when your older brother is the NHL's scoring whiz and star of the day? Well, if you can't beat him at scoring, beat him at everything else.

That is just what Henri Richard, brother of Maurice and fifteen years his junior, did. By the Rocket's own admission, Henri was a better all-around player, except when it came to scoring.

Maurice Richard was the Rocket, so his smaller and younger brother was dubbed "The Pocket Rocket." They also had a brother who failed to stick when he joined the Canadiens; he briefly carried the nickname "The Vest Pocket Rocket." Thank goodness Mère Richard didn't have more hockey-playing boys or things would have just gotten silly. The Ball Of Lint That Gets Stuck to the Kleenex Under Your Wallet in Your Vest Pocket Rocket.

Henri Richard was steady contributor to the Canadiens for twenty years. He carried a record eleven Stanley Cups to the Habs' trophy case. Only former Boston Celtic basketballer Bill Russell can claim as many professional sports championships in North America.

8. Jean Beliveau: Gentleman Hockey Player and Family Man

Jean Beliveau played for the Canadiens for eighteen years and won ten Stanley Cups. He captained five of those ten championship teams. On off days and throughout the summer, he would work at team owner Molson Breweries. In 1994 he was offered the position of governor general, but he declined. Was this guy Canadian or what?

Imagine. You are captain of the Stanley Cup–winning Montreal Canadiens and when you're not playing you work for Molson! Beliveau's face should grace our currency. His name should be worked into the national anthem. There should be a national holiday in his honor sometime during the playoffs. Young Canadians should learn his number, career statistics, and birth date somewhere in between the alphabet and reading.

But I digress …

Beliveau was, in fact, a player and playmaker whose talents were later echoed by the likes of Mario Lemieux. He had a similar uncanny ability to read and anticipate the play. A tough yet clean player, his penalty total runs a close second to his points total (1,029 minutes and 1,219 points). Beliveau was a gentleman who played and worked with dignity.

9. Doug Harvey: I Did It My Way

Doug Harvey did what few other players are able to do: he changed the way the game of hockey was played. When he entered the NHL, the prevailing wisdom when playing the puck in your own zone was to have the forwards fall back to support the puck-carrying defenseman. As that defenseman, Harvey instead had his forwards stay farther up-ice, and he hung around near his own goal for a bit. This tempted the opposing forwards to advance, whereupon Harvey would sneak the puck past them to his waiting teammates, who would then stage a swift rush into their opponents' zone. Some onlookers felt that he was being a little lazy, but they couldn't argue with the results. Harvey collected seven Norris Trophies (awarded for all-around ability as a defenseman) and six Stanley Cups during his career.

Fourteen of his twenty NHL seasons were played with the Montreal Canadiens (1947 to 1961). The devastating Montreal power play of which he was a part led NHL officials to make a significant rule change in 1957. Prior to the change, a player serving a two-minute penalty was required to serve the full two minutes regardless of how many goals the other team scored. After the change, the penalty was over once a goal was awarded. Rules for the entire league changed because one team was so good when playing with the man advantage that it was deemed unfair.

10. Larry Robinson: Here's to You, Mr. Robinson

The best offense is a good defense, they say. The best defense is 6'4" 220-pound Larry Robinson. His was called "Big Bird" for his size, not his demeanor. Plant yourself in front of his goalie, and Number 19 would move you along. He was kind of like a bouncer in a biker bar, only more intimidating.

Intimidating, yes, but not mean. Robinson grew up on a farm in Marvelville, Ontario, and had a quiet strength that was respected on ice and off. Skating into the middle of a scrum, he could calm the situation without resorting to heavy-handed tactics. He was one of what seems to be a dying breed in the NHL, the gentleman player.

Part of six Stanley Cup–winning Canadien teams in his twenty-year career, Larry Robinson played in 227 playoff games, second only to Mark Messier. He rounded out his playing years with the L.A. Kings.

Dave "Tiger" Williams: Honorable (?) Mention

Call it flare, call it style, call it common assault. Call it what you will, Tiger Williams played the game his way, as evidenced by the 4,421 penalty minutes that he served during his fourteen years in professional hockey. That's equivalent to three days straight in the penalty box. In between penalties, Williams spent his time wreaking havoc on behalf of the Toronto Maple Leafs, the Vancouver Canucks, the Detroit Red Wings, the L.A. Kings, and finally the Hartford Whalers. Tiger did not respond well to authority. He still doesn't.

In 1997, a small New Brunswick community announced that police would begin strict enforcement of an existing law that forbade any blockage of town streets. Such offenses included the playing of street hockey. Police, it was said, would fine offenders, and even confiscate nets. A public outcry arose. How dare they threaten a cherished Canadian institution?! Public opinion strongly supported the kids. Street hockey is one of those rare activities that spans generations.

News of the proposed crackdown spread until it made the national news. It was then that a voice was heard from the other side of the country. It was Tiger, and he was pissed. Williams vowed that, if any kid was fined for playing street hockey, he himself would pay the fine. Furthermore, he suggested that when he was a kid and his game was interrupted by an unwelcome motorist, well, let's just say fenders would pay the price.

I salute Dave "Tiger" Williams here, if not for his playing style or personal ethics, for his spirit and love of the game, even at its most basic levels.

> **Bruce:**
> Nothing much else to say in this chapter. Let's skip on ahead to the next chapter. Neato trivia bits in there. Just go on ahead ...

> **Will:**
> Hey, back off Hab-freak! The people need to know the truth!

> **Teena:**
> What is wrong with you guys?

Here It Is! At Last! The World's First Hab-Free Top Ten List

(courtesy of Will "The Oilers Rule(d)" Ferguson)

The first lesson in being a sports fan is this: who you hate is just as important as who you love. And I hate—I absolutely loathe—the Montreal Canadiens. Not only are Habs fans smug, they dwell in the past. The distant past. Habs fans are still swaggering over wins made back in the horse-and-buggy days when there were only six teams vying for the Stanley Cup and the pucks were made of frozen horse poop. Or in the 1940s, when the war had depleted the ranks of hockey; while other young men were fighting overseas to save democracy, the Montreal Canadiens were winning hockey games. Big hairy deal.

> **Bruce:**
> oh please. Do you expect us to believe that the Canadiens refused to join the "... other young men ... fighting overseas to save democracy ..." (want some crackers with that cheese?) so that they could stay home to play hockey?

> And if the entire league suffered from a lack of players during the war; how does that diminish the Canadiens' wins in particular? Have some more grapes, Will. oh, and careful, they're a little sour.

Or the Disco '70s, when the entire league was tilted in their favor and they were allowed to hog the young players coming up. (Today, the lower-ranked teams get first pick, which creates greater equity and makes it very difficult to dominate the game.) Simple truth: The Oilers of the 1980s were the last great hockey dynasty. No one has come close to their record. Certainly not the Canadiens. Here then, is the world's first Top Ten Players' List without a Single Stinkin' Hab Anywhere. These are the *real* top ten of hockey:

Bruce:
What color is the sky in your world, Will?

1. Wayne Gretzky

Career: 1979–99. The Great One. "Gretz" (as he is known to stalker-like fans such as myself) led the Edmonton Oilers to four Stanley Cups before being traded to the L.A. Kings and later the St. Louis Blues. He last played for the New York Rangers and, although a veteran, he was consistently in the top of the standings (in 1998 he was the highest-scoring Canadian player in the NHL). A skinny kid from Brantford, Ontario, Gretzky is not the fastest skater or the strongest, or the hardest shooter. What he has is an uncanny sense of strategy. He has a sixth sense about the flow of the game. Other players look to where the puck is; Gretzky looks for where it *will* be. Simply put, he is the greatest ever to grace us with his presence. A god among men, the people's champion, humble, stalwart, hard-working, selfless, the very epitome of all that is glorious and pure in the——

Bruce:
Enough already

2. Gordie Howe

Career span: 1946–80. Mr. Hockey. When Gordie Howe skated out for one period with the IHL Detroit Vipers on October 3, 1997, he became the first person ever to play professional sports in six separate decades. He was sixty-nine years old. A man of remarkable longevity, Howe was also one of the most dependable players ever. Gordie Howe turned pro in 1945; he led the Detroit Red Wings to four Stanley Cup victories; and at an age when other players were slowing down, Gordie just kept coming. The Energizer Bunny of Hockey. In a sport where thirty-two is old, Gordie Howe played the entire eighty-game season with the Hartford Whalers in 1979–80 and scored fifteen goals—at the age of fifty-two! Although he retired in 1980, he came back for that final game in 1997. Watch out for 2000. We may see Gordie suit up once more for the impossible.

3. Mario Lemieux

Career span: 1984–97. Super Mario. Mario might have gone down as the greatest player ever had his career not been cut short by Hodgkin's disease. While Gretzky was the playmaker, Mario was a scoring machine. He led the Pittsburgh Penguins to back-to-back Stanley Cups in '91 and '92, and the team seemed poised on the brink of greatness. But no. Bad luck, poor management, and a faltering Lemieux ended the dream. In points-per-game average, his record stands virtually neck-and-neck with Gretzky's, and when he was forced to retire he was the top-ranked player in the NHL. Who knows how far Super Mario might have gone?

4. Bobby Orr

Career span: 1966–78. The Killer B. A high-scoring offensive defensemen, Bobby Orr singlehandedly changed how the game was played. While leading the Boston Bruins to two Stanley Cups, Orr perfected the dramatic end-to-end rush that freed defensemen everywhere from the confines of their own end. Gordie Howe himself ranked Orr as the most talented player in the game, and goalie great Jacques Plante agrees. When Orr got hold of a puck, it was magic to watch; he could dip and doodle and deke wave after wave of defensemen out of their shorts. He once scored a Stanley Cup–winning goal more or less in mid-air, after being upended by a St. Louis player in the 1970 final. A classy, clean-cut boy from Parry Sound, Ontario, Orr had the misfortune of playing during hockey's goon era, and his career was cut short by knee injuries.

5. Mark Messier

Career span: 1979–present. The Moose. (Also known as, "The Number 11 Bus.") If scientists ever set out to clone the Perfect Hockey Player, they would create Mark Messier. Together with Gretzky, Messier led the 1980s Oilers to four Stanley Cups and then, just to chasten doubters, won one more after Gretzky was gone. Mark was later traded to the New York Rangers, where he led the team to their first Stanley Cup in more than fifty years. That brings Messier's total to six, proving that the Moose just may be the most important "franchise player" in the league (i.e., a player who makes a team work). Now that Messier has been traded to the Vancouver Canucks, who knows, we may yet see a West Coast Stanley Cup parade.

6. Mike Bossy

Career span: 1977–87. Leader of the powerhouse New York Islanders during their four-year Stanley Cup reign, Mike Bossy, like the Islanders dynasty, has been vastly underrated. If I were playing street hockey, I'd take Bossy over Lafleur any day. Although born in Montreal, Bossy had the good sense not to play for the dwindling Montreal Canadiens—and that alone ranks him high in my eyes. Bossy broke Rocket Richard's record of fifty goals in fifty games, and he did it in a much more competitive league than did Richard. The Stealth Bomber of hockey, Mike Bossy, quietly, carefully, and with almost perfect precision scored the goals that mattered and led his beloved Islanders to four consecutive Stanley Cup championships.

7. Bobby Hull

Career span: 1957–80. The Golden Jet. An outspoken, blond superstar from small-town Ontario, Bobby Hull was as lethal as he was dashing. He had a blistering slapshot—the fastest ever recorded, at 118 miles (190 km) per hour. Although Gordie Howe is heralded as hockey's longest-playing star, Hull's remarkable career span is no less impressive. With the Chicago Blackhawks, Hull won a Stanley Cup, but later left the NHL entirely to become the premier star of the fledgling WHA, where he played first for the Winnipeg Jets, and later with the Hartford Whalers. Bobby's son Brett became a superstar in his own right, making them the first ever father–son combination to win the Hart Trophy. Talk about hockey genes.

8. Bryan Trottier

Career span: 1975–94. Bryan Trottier of Val Marie, Saskatchewan (population: 250), was a multitalented player who could play both tight defensive games and wide-open fire-wagon bouts. The Islanders' all-time point leader, he was anchor of their four-year dynasty. Ignobly dumped by the Islanders after fifteen years of service, he showed the world his true value by joining Super Mario and the Pittsburgh Penguins, and adding two more Stanley Cup rings to his collection. Like Bossy, Trottier has been largely undervalued. A quiet, classy man, never a show-boater, Bryan Trottier was a team player in the best sense of the word.

9. Bobby Clarke

Career span: 1969–84. The meanest player ever to come out of Flin Flon, Manitoba, Bobby Clarke spearheaded the Philadelphia Flyers' brawling four-year, two–Stanley Cup romp. Although the Flyers have gone down in history as the nastiest, brawlingest team ever, they didn't win solely on goon power. Bobby Clarke was the hardest-working player ever, a dogged player who gave every game his all and who overcame diabetes to become one of the best team captains ever. Arguably one of the best penalty killers ever—and playing with the Philadelphia Flyers he had to be—Clarke was one of the game's dirtiest players. He embodied the best and worst that hockey in the 1970s had to offer.

10. Ray Bourque

Career span: 1979–present. Although he has never won a Stanley Cup, I included Ray Bourque on the top ten because he was such an exciting player to watch. For the last twenty years, Bourque has been the heart and soul of the Boston Bruins, one of the best defensemen ever—second, perhaps, only to Bobby Orr himself. Acknowledged as one of the best technicians in the game, Bourque is second only to Gordie Howe, with seventeen straight all-star selections. Like Mike Bossy, Bourque has never had the success he deserved. The Bruins should have had a half-dozen Stanley Cups since Bourque joined them, but as a team they seem condemned to always finish just short of a final victory. *Always a bridesmaid, never a bride.*

Teena's Picks

Now that you've read the boys' long-winded vows of eternal love and faith, it's time to learn about the really important players. I'd like to introduce you to the Top Ten Handsomest Players in the NHL. I have done exhaustive, grueling research, hours of staring at magazines, glaring, squinting, and fantasizing to bring you this exclusive list. I've worked late into the night, reviewing this list with a select panel of experts (my sister and my girlfriends) to validate my choices of the choicest.

1. Steve Yzerman: No. 19 Detroit Red Wings

Ladies, we have a winner. Steve Yzerman (or as I like to call him, My Sweet Stevie Y) is *the* most handsome Babe-o-la in the NHL. Think of any

fantasy in your repertoire and you can cast Stevie as the leading man. He is so pretty he could have been a model. If I had one NHL Rules wish it is that Handsome Steve would have to play hockey wearing full body armor or at the very least a goalie's mask and a titanium cup.

Yzerman isn't just a pretty face, though; he was drafted by the Detroit Red Wings in 1983 and has been their captain since 1986. He was born on May 9, 1965, in Cranbrook, British Columbia. This 5'11", 180-pound Hunka-Hunka-Burnin'-Love has also won the Lester B. Pearson Award and two Stanley Cups. Sweet Stevie was the youngest player (age eighteen) to play in a NHL All Star game. He's handsome, incredibly talented, and a millionaire. Who could ask for anything more?

2.   Alexandre Daigle: No. 11 Philadelphia Flyers

Steve Yzerman may be the most handsome player in the NHL, but, at the tender age of twenty-three, Alexandre Daigle is the NHL stud. Yzerman is handsome, but Daigle is hot.

Daigle was born on February 7, 1975, in Montreal, Quebec. He was the number one draft choice in the 1993 entry draft, was signed by the Ottawa Senators, and now plays right wing for the Philadelphia Flyers. He is a solid, clean player.

This 6', 200-pound hip-cat prefers Armani and Versace clothing, and his favorite color is black. Daigle is too cool for hockey. He likes Italian food, rock music, Richard Gere, and Cameron Diaz.

3.   Mark Messier: No. 11 Vancouver Canucks

Imagine, it's the third period, the clock is ticking, the game is tied, the pressure is on, and Mark Messier gets a five-minute major. He heads off to the hot, steamy penalty box, he's sweaty and full of adrenaline, and there you are, hiding in the box to help those five minutes pass.

One look at those "I'm up to something devilish" eyes and his salesman's "Trust me" grin and you know what Mark Messier is: a bad, *bad* boy.

Mark Messier was born on January 18, 1961, in Edmonton, Alberta into a hockey family (his dad is Doug Messier). Picked up by the WHA at the tender age of seventeen, Mark was noticed by Glen Sather, coach of the Edmonton Oilers. It wasn't his scoring abilities that caught Sather's attention (Messier had only one goal in the fifty-two games he played with the WHA), but the fact that he beat up one of Sather's Oilers players. Edmonton drafted him the following year and since his 1979 draft this 6'1", 210-pound bruiser has won six Stanley Cups and has been the captain for the Edmonton Oilers, captain of the New York Rangers, and captain of the Vancouver Canucks.

Mark Messier is also a generous and giving bad boy. He has raised more than $600,000 for the Tomorrow's Children's Fund and often brings children to practices and games.

Mark Messier is an amazing player. He's rough and hard, and that's how we like him. All this bad boy really needs is a spanking.

4. Eric Lindros: No. 88 Philadelphia Flyers

It's a late autumn afternoon, the air is crisp, you can smell the falling leaves and the wood being split in the backyard of your mountain cabin. You watch him swing the ax, his square jaw set, a day's scruff growing on his face, his intense eyes determined, his curly brown hair feathering softly in the breeze, and a warm wool sweater holding him. This is how *I* like to imagine Eric Lindros. A lot of people imagine him differently: some picture him hurt, others much worse. Eric Lindros is not for everyone. In fact you can find websites entitled "Why I Hate Eric Lindros" and a booing section anywhere he plays. Of course, all of this is unfair. Eric is just a misunderstood giant.

Lindros was born on February 28, 1973, in London, Ontario. He was drafted by the Quebec Nordiques in 1991 and then traded to the Philadelphia Flyers. He is known as one of the NHL's "big men," at 6'4", 240 pounds. In fact some players claim the digging of his skate blades into the ice sounds louder than normal. Lindros uses this to his advantage. He once told an opposing player, "Listen for me, you'll hear me coming."

I'm listening.

5. Jaromir Jagr: No. 68 Pittsburgh Penguins

Long, curly black hair catching the wind, tuxedo tastefully taut across his wide shoulders and broad chest, a bottle of red wine in one hand, a wildflower in the other, and the sun descending on the beach behind him— this is how you want to see Jaromir Jagr.

Jagr was born on February 15, 1972, in Kladno, Czech Republic (young *and* European). He was the first Czechoslovakian player to attend the NHL draft without having to defect. He was drafted by the Pittsburgh

Penguins in 1990 and remains there today as their right-winger. In fact, he holds the NHL single-season record for most points by a right-winger. He's also won two Stanley Cups and the Art Ross Trophy. Jagr is known as the best "one on one" player in the league (young, European, and into monogamy). His personal record is three goals per game (young, European, monogamous, and can score three times a night!).

Jaromir Jagr is a humble man. He enjoys listening to music, tennis, traveling, and reading Czechoslovakian history.

6.   Paul Kariya: No. 9 Anaheim Mighty Ducks

Poor Paul Kariya. This sweet little guy needs to be kept in bed for about a week with his head safely in a pillow. He should be cuddled, stroked, and loved in his jammies. This adorably handsome young player keeps getting bonked in the head by big, bad hockey bullies.

At 5'11", 180 pounds, Paul is one of the smaller players in the league. He was born in Vancouver, British Columbia, on October 16, 1974. While growing up, people told him that he might not have a NHL career because of his size. This didn't upset him because the NHL became his second dream; his first dream was to play in the Olympics. He proved size didn't matter (in this case) when he was drafted by Anaheim in 1993, but staying true to his dreams, Kariya put off his draft until he could play in the 1994 Olympic Winter Games. The gold medal that year came down to a shootout between Canada and Sweden. Kariya was chosen for the shootout and lost, giving the gold to Sweden and the silver to Canada. Poor Paul was disappointed but went back to play for Anaheim, where in the last few years has proven to be one of the top NHL players.

When the 1998 Winter Olympics announced that professional players were allowed to play in the games, Paul Kariya was a shoo-in. He was ready to make up for that missed shot in the last Olympics, and as he is of Japanese descent, Japan was excited to receive him. Then, on a dark and stormy night, just before the Olympics, in a game against the Chicago Blackhawks, Paulie scored a goal and was promptly hit by the evil Chicago defenseman Gary Suter. Paul suffered a concussion, one of many in his early career, and the evil Suter suffered a four-game suspension that did not apply to the Olympics. Suter got to play with Team U.S.A. in Nagano, and Kariya got to play with a bottle of aspirin in bed.

Paul Kariya is a good, clean player. He has already twice won the Lady Byng Memorial Trophy for gentlemanly play. Young, talented, and handsome, he's the kind of player I like to see on the ice—or, for that matter, in my shower.

7. Chris Chelios: No. 24 Detroit Red Wings

Chris Chelios is the dark knight of the NHL. He is an intense defenseman, though "intense" may be an understatement; he has had 2,000 penalty minutes in his career. Many people in the league hate him: Chelios is known to often use his stick as a scythe and, to some, he looks like Death in skates.

It is true that Chelios is an aggressive player who hates to lose, even during team scrimmages. ESPN analyst Bill Clement once observed that "a lot of people fight for the puck, Chris plays like he's fighting for his life." Obviously this passion has worked for Chelios. He's played in the Olympics twice (1984 and 1998), won the Norris Trophy three times, and owns a Stanley Cup Champion's ring. Chris Chelios is the most skilled and scary defenseman in the NHL, but that is only one side of this 6'1", 190-pound brute.

Chelios is also involved in his community and gives freely with his giant, brutish heart. He raises money for underprivileged kids through his foundation, "Cheli's Children," and owns a bar/restaurant named "Cheli's Chili."

Chris Chelios isn't menacing or mean, he's just driven and passion-ate—and he can drive to my place and show me his passion any time.

8. Brett Hull: No. 22 Dallas Stars

A handsome, fair-haired angel, Brett Hull is the kind of guy you'd love to marry. You can see this 5'11", 200-pound cutie fresh out of the shower, wrapped in a towel, holding a baby, the picture of manhood and sensitivity.

Born on August 9, 1964, in Belleville, Ontario, Brett was drafted in 1984 by the Calgary Flames. He has since been traded to the St. Louis Blues, where he was the captain and now plays right wing. Brett comes from a hockey family; his uncle is Dennis Hull, who played for the Chicago Blackhawks and the Detroit Red Wings, and his father is Hockey Hall of Famer Bobby Hull. He's won the Hart Memorial Trophy and the Lester B. Pearson Award. Sweet Brett also won the Lady Byng Memorial Trophy for gentlemanly conduct in play.

Now don't let all this niceness fool you. Brett Hull is rumored to be an "excellent passer" and to have "great hands." He is also quite the scorer, at 500. If you are the jealous type, he may not be for you.

The Gardens

Les Habitants

Nos Glorieux

The Sentors

9. Brendan Shanahan: No 14 Detroit Red Wings

Take one look at those soft, brown, puppy-dog eyes and you will fall for Shanny.

Brendan Shanahan is no puppy on the ice, though. This big left-winger can rough it up. He was born in Mimico, Ontario, on January 23, 1969. Drafted in 1987 by the New Jersey Devils, Shanahan was traded to the St. Louis Blues, and then to the Harford Whalers, where he was captain. He now plays with the Detroit Red Wings. Since being with the Wings, Shanny has helped them win two Stanley Cups.

Brendan Shanahan enjoys indoor lacrosse, watching movies, and Italian food. His favorite vacation spot is France, where he usually travels alone. Alone—as in, without a girlfriend. He is *single*.

10. Don Sweeney: No. 32 Boston Bruins

I did not pick Don because he is from my home town. I did not pick Don because he happens to be the only NHL player whose body has actually caressed mine. I picked Don Sweeney for his square, manly jaw line; his wide, handsome grin; and those smiling eyes.

Now that I've defended myself I'll give you the sordid details. Don was born on August 17, 1966, in St. Stephen, New Brunswick, where I was born and schooled. Mr. "Just Look at My Grin" Sweeney spoke at my high-school graduation and he looked hot up on that stage. Being one of the artistically talented students (aka Flake, Weirdo, Freak of Nature), I helped to design and make a thank-you gift for our star speaker. The gift was a special box of chocolates, with my cover design, "Sweeney Sweets." Yes, it was lame, but I got to give a welcome speech, had my photo taken with a hockey babe, and managed to cop a quick grope. Technically, the grope was a hug, but to a sex-starved, never-had-a-boyfriend, angst-ridden, teenaged girl it was practically a proposition.

Our young love affair aside, Don is a wonderful defenseman for Boston. He was drafted by the Bruins in 1984 and before that went to Harvard. This 5'10", 188-pound suave sophisticate makes a bundle, some of which he has been saving for a trip to Paris with me so we can rediscover our lost love. He'll probably be calling with the flight number soon.

11

Why is the Puck Black?

... and Other Nagging Questions

Why is the puck black?

The puck is black because during the manufacturing process carbon black (coal dust) is added to the rubber. Black seems like a boring color for such a busy piece of equipment. It's true that black on white is high contrast, but since other equipment and parts of the players' uniforms are black, it can be confusing. Imagine if the puck was bright purple, lime green, or even fluorescent orange. The game would be much easier to follow. Colored pucks have been used before. The now disbanded WHA used orange ones. The problem with colored pucks, however, is that they chip and don't hold their shape. So, girls, we're stuck with basic boring, black chunks of frozen rubber. Unless we watch hockey on Fox.

How does the FoxTrax puck work?

The FoxTrax puck makes following the puck easier. Fox Broadcasting developed a computerized puck that glows on the television screen and has a little tail that looks like a comet. The puck appears blue until it reaches 65 miles (104 km) per hour, then it turns red.

Some hockey purists hate the FoxTrax puck and feel that, if you can't follow the traditional black puck, then you are not worthy of hockey fandom. Whatever.

The FoxTrax does make the game easier to follow and it looks cute buzzing around the screen. Fox created this effect by slicing a traditional NHL puck in half, hollowing it out slightly, installing a tiny circuit board and a series of diodes inside, and then gluing the puck back together. Sensors are installed above the rinks where the FoxTrax is used. These sensors send the puck information to computers. The computers send the info to the Fox "Puck Truck," a mobile production vehicle that sends the FoxTrax to us.

Being pro or anti FoxTrax decides what style of a hockey fan you are—Purist or Evolutionist.

Who came up with that theme song for "Hockey Night in Canada"?

You've heard it. It's practically the national anthem for our guys. I bet if you asked your guy to sing "O Canada" he'd stare at you blankly. But start humming the theme to "Hockey Night in Canada" and he's at attention, eyes bright, nodding his head in tempo. Dah … Dah … Dum union.

This theme was composed by Dolores Clayman-Morris in the 1960s while she was working for a Toronto jingle company, Quartet Productions. The producers of "Hockey Night in Canada" approached the company to create a bold theme for hockey. Dolores received a lump-sum payment for the first five years of use of the song, but after that period, receives royalties each time it is used. Not bad for a jingle.

What are the players saying on the ice?

Girlfriend, you don't want to know what they are saying. Not if you have delicate ears or didn't grow up near a loading dock. These boys on ice have potty-mouths. Nothing is sacred when it comes to insults; players often question the opposition's family lineage, make comments about the player's mother or sister or wife, or even (gasp!) their girlfriend.

Why such a lack of brotherly love and camaraderie? Simple. The players are trying to get the opposition angry so they'll take a stupid penalty or at least break their concentration for a moment.

Teammates also talk to each other on the ice. They ask for the puck or warn against the oncoming opposition. The player doing the most yelling is the goalie. From his vantage he can see the whole game, allowing him to scream directions to the players, telling the defense to move out of his way or the forwards what to do when they are behind the net. The players learn to recognize their teammates' voices; otherwise, a crafty player from the opposition could fool them.

King Clancy once pulled this trick on hockey's first tough guy, Sprague Cleghorn. Cleghorn was heading toward Clancy's net with only one man between him and a goal. King Clancy was trailing behind him, when a bright idea struck him. Clancy tapped his stick on the ice and yelled Cleghorn's name. Sprague Cleghorn thought Clancy was his teammate and passed the puck back to him. The giggling Clancy got the puck and headed to the other end of the ice. Cleghorn was pissed! After the game, while heading to the dressing room, Clancy heard his name being called. He turned around to greet his enthusiastic fans but instead met Sprague Cleghorn's fist!

The linesmen and referee hear a lot of talking, most of which is bologna. Players try to play innocent when called for a penalty or argue the punishment; sometimes they even tattle on other players, trying to squeeze out a penalty for the opposition or at least plant a seed of doubt in the referee's mind. Referees and linesmen also have to put up with a lot of insults from the coaches and fans. These insults usually relate to visual acuity. (In most arenas there is a ban on playing "Three Blind Mice" when the ref or linesmen make a bad call.)

The television microphones often miss the colorful language of hockey. Fortunately, the camera doesn't. If you are interested in hockey dirty talk, learn to lip-read. It's not that hard; you have only a few choice words to learn.

Why doesn't the referee break up a fight sooner?

Sometimes a ref will allow a brouhaha to continue for a few seconds. I hate fighting in hockey, so if you listen carefully during one of these allowed episodes you will hear me yelling, "Break it up, you twit. What? Are you blind? They're beating the bejesus out of each other!" In a perfect world (my world), a player would be called the moment he cocked his fist. But this is not a perfect world, and sometimes brief fisticuffs are allowed. The referee does have a reason for this. If a fight breaks out between two tough players and the officials feel it would help settle the game down, they will allow the tango to continue for a moment. If it is an uneven fight, or has a chance of getting out of control, the ref will stop it immediately.

What do players do to stay in shape?

Sex, sex, sex, and more sex.

Okay, maybe this isn't the training program for most hockey players (but I hope it's Messier's). Most players are constantly conditioning for the game. Some only take about two weeks off at the end of the season. A typical hockey training program includes cycling, the Stairmaster, weightlifting, and, of course, skating. Hockey players do exercises that are gentle on the knees and back (players' most injured and abused areas) and build strength and stamina.

What do players eat before a game?

In general, hockey players eat a lot. They have to because they burn a lot of calories on ice. Traditionally, players ate a steak before the game; now the pre-game dish is often pasta. They also drink a lot of water or fruit juice with their pre-game meal so their bodies have a good fluid supply going into the game.

Why can't the players play with their teeth in? Please?

I know, they look like hillbillies, but we can't be selfish. If the players played with their faux choppers, they could have them knocked loose and choke on them.

Where are their teeth? The first set was probably sucked up by the Zamboni or is still stuck in someone's stick. During a game the players keep their false set in the dressing room in little cups.

Why are there so few black hockey players?

The history of black players in the NHL has been a tough one. The story of black players begins (or didn't begin, I should say) with Herb Carnegie. Herb was an excellent player in the Junior A league in Toronto during the 1940s. He was rumored to be the best center-ice man in the nation. He won three MVP awards and hoped to break into the NHL, but he didn't, because he was black and no one would sign a black player in those days.

It wasn't until 1958 that an NHL team drafted a black player, when Willie O'Ree, a rookie from Fredericton, New Brunswick, was drafted by the Boston Bruins. But O'Ree's NHL career wasn't long: he played forty-five games, scoring four goals, and was sent back to the minor league, never to return.

The next black players were Mike Marson and Bill Riley, who joined the Washington Capitals in the 1970s, but their careers were short as well.

Tony McKegney, from Sarnia, Ontario, was the first black player to have a full NHL career. McKegney was drafted by the Buffalo Sabres in 1978, he scored 320 goals in his 912 NHL games and played for eight different teams. Grant Fuhr, the once unbeatable Oilers goalie in the 1980s, was probably the most famous black player.

Why are our hockey guys so obsessed with hockey cards? What do those letters and numbers on the back of the card mean?

Most of our guys, at some point in their lives, have collected hockey cards. I'm sure you've heard the story of how your guy had Gordie Howe's rookie card but his thoughtless mother threw it out, or, worse, threw out his whole collection when he moved into his first bachelor pad. The hockey guy will obsess for hours over his lost collection and how valuable it was. Why? Maybe it's a fond-childhood-memory thing, or maybe hockey guys are just obsessive by nature.

I decided that hockey cards were a part of the hockey culture that I didn't understand and needed to experience. So off to the local grocery store Bruce and I went to buy my initiatory hockey cards. I was a hockey-card virgin, and it was kind of exciting. I had an unopened packet with a surprise inside. The anticipation built as I opened the package, wondering who I'd get. But when I shuffled the cards, none of them were for my favorite handsome guys, so it was over. I then made a hockey *faux pas*: I gathered the cards (mine and Bruce's) into *one* pile and went to put them away. Bruce froze and stared at me like I had just spit at the Stanley Cup.

"You mixed them up!" he said, dazed.

"Oh, I don't care. You can have mine."

That was my second hockey-card faux pas. You see, the whole point of hockey cards is: (a) possession and (b) trading.

"I'm not buying you any more hockey cards," said Bruce officiously. "You are cut off."

I managed to patch things up and, the next time I bought cards, I got some of my players and Bruce got Mark Messier. This is where I discovered the fun of hockey cards. I wanted that Messier card. After some tough but futile bargaining and a long tickle fight, I had the Messier card tucked safely in my bra. Girls, all is fair in love, war, and hockey-card trading. So what you trade yours for is up to you.

Whom do we thank for hockey cards? We can trace card collecting back to 1910, when cigarette companies first issued them. Thirteen years later, candy companies were following suit. In 1930, the St. Lawrence Starch Company began a label mail-in promotion with their corn syrup that allowed people to collect photos of the Toronto Maple Leafs and the Montreal Canadiens. By 1939, you could collect player photos from all six NHL teams. The corn syrup promotion was suspended in 1968, when the NHL demanded too much money for the rights to the player photos.

Hockey cards more famously came with dry, rock-hard bubble gum. Nowadays, the cards are usually alone in the package because the gum can damage the card's value.

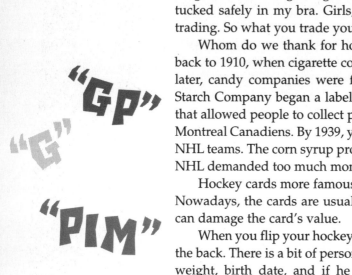

When you flip your hockey card over you, will find some statistics on the back. There is a bit of personal information on the player—his height, weight, birth date, and if he shoots right or left. You will also find columns of numbers with lettered headings that seem to be a chemical recipe for nuclear fission. I am here to demystify those numbers for you. The stats correspond, in a row, to the year the player played and for what team. The abbreviations mean: *GP*—games played; *G*—goals; *A*—assists; *PTS*—points (goals and assists added together); *PIM*—penalties in minutes; *PPG*—power play goals; +/——this number represents the goals scored when the player is on the ice (if his team gets a goal when he is on the ice, then he is +1, if the opposition scores while he is on the ice, then he is –1).

These stats are usually followed by a paragraph summarizing the player's career and special talents (non-sexual, alas).

What is up with those nicknames?

There are some cool hockey nicknames, Curtis Joseph's "Cujo" is scary (you want to imagine a crazy, rabid dog lurking in the goal net) and the "Dominator" (Dominik Hasek) is very intimidating. But then there are some really lame nicknames. I've sorted through the various peculiar and sometimes perplexing names to bring you my:

Top Ten Stupid Hockey Nicknames

10. "**Big Bird**" Is this an image a goalie would find intimidating—a giant yellow bird skating at him, trying to teach him the ABCs? This was Larry Robinson's nickname. "Big Bird" played for the Montreal Canadiens and the Los Angeles Kings, where he retired in 1992.

9. "**Gump**" Lorne Worsley is actually known and listed in record books as "Gump," not by his given name. He played for the Montreal Canadiens, New York Rangers, and the Minnesota North Stars before he retired in 1974.

8. "**Le Canard**" (the Duck). What is it with hockey players and yellow fuzzy birds? Do they all share some common childhood phobia? "The Duck" was Montreal Canadiens' player Réjean Houle, who retired in 1983.

7. "**Cement Head**" This flattering nickname belongs to Dave Semenko, who played for the Edmonton Oilers, Hartford Whalers, and the Toronto Maple Leafs. "Cement Head" retired in 1988.

6. "**Flower Power**" "Flower" is a direct translation of his name (Guy Lafleur) and it was the 1970s, but couldn't anyone think of a more daunting and less dainty nickname? Pretty "Flower" played for the Montreal Canadiens, New York Rangers, and the Quebec Nordiques before ending his seventeen-year career in 1991.

5. Frank "**Seldom**" Beaton. Now, there is a name that inspires confidence! Mr. Beaton played for the New York Rangers and retired in 1980.

4. Larry "**Izzy**" Goodenough. With a name like Goodenough, he had to expect this when he first dreamed of the NHL. "Izzy" played for the Philadelphia Flyers and the Vancouver Canucks until his retirement in 1980.

3. "**Puck-goes-Inski**" This terrible nickname belongs to New York Ranger's goalie Steve Buzinski. Steve played nine games for New York and allowed fifty-five goals before he "retired" in 1943.

2. "**Bluet Bionic**" (the Bionic Blueberry). This one is too bizarre. It belongs to Mario Tremblay, who played for the Montreal Canadiens until 1986.

1. "**The Chicoutimi Cucumber**" Georges Vézina hailed from Chicoutimi, Quebec, and apparently, on ice, was as cool as a cucumber. A cuke! Not one person in the NHL could think of a cooler image than a long, green vegetable that gives you gas?

Top Ten Stupid Nicknames

Is the Toronto Maple Leafs organization illiterate?

Even the particularities of Canadian spelling can't explain the name of Toronto's team. It should be the Leaves, not the Leafs.

Why such a strange spelling? Because Conn Smythe said it sounded good, and everyone listened. Smythe was among the group of Toronto businessmen who bought the team (then the St. Patricks) and became their coach and manager the following season. The team switched names from the St. Pats to the Leafs shortly after its change of ownership in 1927. Conn Smythe, as legend goes, actually chose the name himself. He claimed that the maple leaf symbol would mean something to all Canadians. Papers began reporting the new team name as the Leafs and illiterate hockey history began.

Why do players shake hands at the end of a game?

I admit it is strange to see players who have just thrashed, beaten, and crushed other players shaking hands (and even giving some of those cute "guy hugs" where they hug with one arm and pound the back with the other) like old buddies. But the fact is some of these players are old buddies. It is a sweet tradition that says all is forgiven. It's quite touching. The big galoots really are just kids at heart.

Why are hockey guys so obsessed with the Zamboni?

The Zamboni is the weird-looking machine that drives around the ice, resurfacing it, between periods.

The Zamboni was invented in the 1940s by Frank Zamboni. Frank was an arena owner in California, who dabbled in mechanics and formerly owned an ice-making factory. Frank knew ice and soon got tired of the long, arduous task of resurfacing it for skaters and hockey players. Before his invention, large drums full of hot water were dragged over the ice on carts, and the water was released through a cloth that hung behind the carts. With the invention of the Zamboni, the ice surface could be scraped, cleaned, and flooded in under ten minutes.

When I asked Bruce why hockey guys loved the Zamboni driver so much, he replied, eyes wide, "Because he gets to drive the car … inside!"

What are all those Trophies they yak about?

Okay, here's a quick rundown.

Art Ross Trophy: Awarded to the player who leads the league in scoring. Gretzky has won it a million times.

Bill Masterton Memorial Trophy: Awarded to the player who displays qualities of perseverance, sportsmanship, and dedication.

Calder Memorial Trophy: Awarded to the outstanding rookie of that NHL season. One of the few trophies Gretzky did *not* win.

Conn Smythe Trophy: Awarded to the most valuable player to his team during the Stanley Cup playoffs.

Frank J. Selke Trophy: Awarded to the forward who excels in the defensive aspects of the game.

Hart Memorial Trophy: Awarded to the player that is the most valuable to his team. Gretzky has won this one about a million times, too.

James Norris Memorial Trophy: Awarded to the player voted best defenseman.

Lady Byng Memorial Trophy: Awarded to a player who has had a season of good clean play and gentlemanly conduct. I'm betting "Bad Boy Marky Messier" will never win this one.

Vezina Trophy: Awarded to the league's best goalie.

These awards are given out at a televised banquet at the end of the season; it's the "Oscars" of the hockey world. This show is worth watching. By the end of the playoffs our sweet players are looking pretty ragged. They are bruised, swollen, bleeding, stitched, unshaven, overtired, and overworked shells of their former handsomeness. For this banquet they have had time to heal, sleep, and shave. They're all dressed up and looking mighty fine!

So, You Think You're Smart, do You?

Impress Your Friends and Loved Ones with Your Newfound Knowledge

By this point you probably think you're quite the smartypants, so full of newfound knowledge that you could involuntarily start to spew hockey facts at any moment. It's time to put this wisdom to good use—namely, to impress and intimidate your hockey guy. The info in this chapter will help you win bets and admiration.

I remember the first time I shocked Will and Bruce with my new hockey knowledge. The boys were yakking on about a game that I was only half-watching when there was a prolonged mixup behind the net. Bruce started muttering about how the game would be faster if the rink was bigger, like it is in European hockey, and Will agreed. I interrupted to correct the commentary. "Actually," I said, "European rinks are wider but not longer." I didn't even realize that one of the many seemingly useless hockey facts I had learned had leaked out of my brain. The boys looked at me with an expression of wounded pride and deep respect. I had corrected them on hockey. It was a sweet moment.

Wee Wayne's Record

Sure, he was great as an adult, but did you know that Wayne Gretzky scored 1,000 goals in minor hockey before he was thirteen?

Hockey Art Critic

During the mid-1980s Andy Warhol asked Wayne Gretzky to pose, in uniform, for a series of lithos. Gretzky agreed, but when the series opened at a posh Manhattan hotel, hockey people were shocked. The artist was interested in the deforming natures of portraiture and had painted a crude sketch of the Great One over which he added a vivid color scheme of dark brown, bright purple, electric blue, and yellow. When asked by a reporter if he liked the paintings, Gretzky moaned, "He didn't even get the Oilers' colors right."

Grandpa Gordie

Hall of Famer Gordie Howe player pro hockey for thirty-two years. In fact, he was on ice the night he became a grandfather.

Lover Lafleur

Guy Lafleur was quite the romantic. Growing up in a small town, Lafleur was a shy guy, and when he arrived in the big city of Montreal he didn't make many friends. His only friend during his first year was his janitor. Lafleur's friend told him about a lovely stewardess who lived in the building. Guy dropped in to the lovely stewardess's apartment and began some small talk. When there was a lull in the conversation, Lafleur quipped, "To go out with me, you have to lose fifty pounds." Needless to say, the lovely stewardess threw Lafleur out on his bloated head. Still, Lafleur wasn't put off. When he knew the stewardess was out one evening, he took the janitor's keys and let himself in to her apartment. He relaxed, had a cognac on her couch, and fell asleep. When the lovely stewardess arrived the next morning to discover Lafleur on her couch, he smiled and said, "You're early," and she again gave him the heave-ho. She was so upset by these antics that the lovely stewardess left Montreal for Quebec City. Guy Lafleur hopped into his car and followed this poor woman to Quebec and confessed that he had been acting so crazy because of … love. Cupid made him do it. The two then returned to Montreal, where, a year later, the lovely stewardess became Lafleur's lovely wife.

Star Studded

Maurice "Rocket" Richard once earned all three stars in a game against Toronto. Richard got a standing ovation for scoring all five goals in the 5-1 victory. If your hockey guy scored five times in one night, I think you'd give him a standing ovation too!

Game Quickie

The shortest game in hockey history happened between the Long Island Ducks and the New Haven Blades in the old Eastern League (before the NHL was formed). The Ducks had a pair of very scary defensemen, John Brophy and Don Perry. Both players played a tough, mean, and painfully physical game. During their first shift against the Blades, Brophy and Perry were doing their usual bump and grind, and they clobbered two of the Blades players. That was enough for the Blades. After just eighty seconds of play, they left the ice and hung up their skates. The Ducks' coach rushed to the visitors dressing room and offered them $100 each to come back on the ice and face his rabid Duckies, but no player would take the chance and all went home.

Hasty Hat Trick

Bill Mosienko of the Chicago Blackhawks scored the fastest hat trick in history in the final game of the 1951–52 season. Chicago was losing to the New York Rangers in the third period of the game when suddenly Bill Mosienko went nuts. Mosienko scored a goal at 6:09, 6:20, and 6:30—three goals in twenty-one seconds! The Blackhawks won the game 7-6.

Rookie Quickie

Gus Bodnar of the Toronto Maple Leafs set a rookie record in the 1943–44 season. Bodnar scored against the New York Rangers fifteen seconds after the opening whistle blew on his first NHL shift.

Starting Scores

The record for the fastest goal from the start of the game is shared by two players: Bryan Trottier of the New York Islanders and Doug Smail of the

Winnipeg Jets. Both of these high-speed studs scored after only five seconds of play.

Ultra-Suspended

Three men have been suspended for life from the NHL. What the hell do you have to do to be suspended for life from a game that encourages players to crush every bone in their opponents' bodies against a four-foot wall and then beat the bejesus out of them?

Bill Coutu of the Boston Bruins was suspended for life in 1927. King Bad Boy Billy was known as a mean-tempered player who would deliver crushing body-checks in games, and even in team scrimmages. Billy was a ten-year veteran when he attacked the wrong guy, a referee. He assaulted referee Jerry Laflamme and then knocked him down. Billy then decided that the linesman needed a butt-kickin' too, so he tackled him as well. Five years later, the suspension was lifted, but Billy Coutu was too old to return to the game.

Billy Taylor of the New York Rangers and Don Gallinger of the Boston Bruins were both suspended for life in 1947 by NHL president Clarence Campbell. Campbell had discovered that these two bad boys were involved with gamblers and placing bets on NHL games. Their suspensions were not lifted until 1970. The bad boys were now middle-aged, but Taylor returned to hockey (coaching and scouting), although Gallinger never did.

Bucko's Bum

You must wonder that in a sport as rough and crazy-fast as hockey there must be some bizarre injuries.

One of the strangest that I have read about is the story of the NHL's biggest pain in the ass. Bucko McDonald was a good defenseman—he could stop plays and punish any player who got too friendly with the goalie—but he had trouble dropping to the ice to block a shot. After being traded from Detroit to Toronto in 1938, Bucko was paired up with the dropping defenseman extraordinaire Bob Goldham. The Leafs' coach hassled Bucko to learn Goldham's falling and blocking tricks, but Bucko couldn't catch on. Finally, Bucko McDonald dropped for a shot. Unfortunately, Bucko had adopted a new style (ignoring the advice of his defense partner to drop into a "half curtsy") and he fell quickly, straight down on both knees. Now, these were the golden years before heel guards, and Bucko had skewered himself in the bum with his own skates. Ouch.

Hockey Love Bites

We all know that some hockey players can fight dirty. They call others names, whack sticks off teeth, trip, and check from behind. But did you know that when the moon rose over Quebec in May 1986 it summoned Hockey Vampires? It happened first during the opening round of the Stanley Cup playoffs when Jimmy Mann of the Quebec Nordiques bit Torrie Robertson of the Hartford Whalers on the cheek. Then during the Cup finals, after initiating a bench-clearing brawl, Claude Lemieux dined on the finger of Calgary Flames' Jim Peplinski. Later Lemieux claimed to the press that he didn't do it, but we all know not to trust the seductive words of a vampire.

The Penalty Cell

Dino Ciccarelli became the first NHL player to be locked up in jail for attacking an opposing player on ice. It happened on August 24, 1988, when Ciccarelli brained Toronto's Luke Richardson (twice over the head with his stick) and then punched him in the mouth. His jailhouse blues only lasted for two hours before he was released.

NHL Death

With a game that is as bone-crushingly fast as hockey, it is hard to believe there has been only one on-ice death in NHL history. It happened in January 13, 1968, during the first year for the Minnesota North Stars (since moved to Dallas as the Stars). The helmetless Bill Masterton of the North Stars was checked by two of the Oakland Seals defensemen; he fell, striking his head on the ice, and later died in hospital from brain injuries.

Hockey Murder?

Though Bill Masterton's was the only death in NHL history, there is another on-ice death. The death of Owen McCourt happened on March 6,

1907 (ten years before the birth of the NHL) in the old Federal League.

McCourt was a leading scorer for the Cornwall, Ontario, team who were playing the Ottawa Vics. During the game, McCourt became involved in a fight with Ottawa's Art Throop, and soon other players joined in. One of the joining players was Ottawa's Charlie Masson. As the brutal brouhaha continued, Masson smashed McCourt over the head with his stick. McCourt dropped to the ice unconscious. He was rushed to the hospital, where he died a few hours later.

Masson was arrested, and many people called it murder and wanted to see him locked up for life. At the trial a few weeks later, there was confusion over whether it was Masson's blow that killed McCourt or the blows from another player, or even a combination of the two. Since the judge was unable to determine which stick killed poor McCourt, Masson was acquitted and released. The Ottawa team was clouded by the death and canceled the rest of their games that season.

Hockey Angels

We always hear about the hockey bad boys, the players who live in the penalty box, but who are the hockey good boys? These are the players who never injure and are never in trouble with the refs, the sweet little hockey angels. Val Fonteyne played from 1959 to 1972 (thirteen years) for the Detroit Red Wings, New York Rangers, and the Pittsburgh Penguins. Fonteyne racked up a record twenty-six penalty minutes—total. That's an average of two minutes a year in the penalty box. The second most innocent hockey angel is Clint Smith. Smith played for the New York Rangers and the Chicago Blackhawks from 1936 to 1947 (eleven years), and totalled just twenty-four penalty minutes in his long career.

Bad, Bad Boy

Randy Holt was in a bad, bad, mood on March 11, 1979. It was a game between Holt's team, the Los Angeles Kings, and the Philadelphia Flyers. The poor object of Holt's mood was Frank Bathe of the Flyers. Holt was a one-man demolition team; he racked up nine penalties and sixty-seven penalty minutes, setting an NHL record. He collected one minor, three majors, two ten-minute misconducts, and three game misconducts, all in the opening period! Bathe, who had been hammering it out with Holt in the first period, ended the game with the second-highest single-game penalty minutes, an amazing (and terrifying) fifty-five minutes. The records for first- and second-highest penalty minutes were set in one scary, and painful, game.

Holt still holds the record for most penalty minutes in a game, but on March 31, 1991, Chris Nilan of the Boston Bruins broke his record for actual number of penalties in a game. Nilan tallied ten penalties in a game against Hartford.

Penguin Pneumonia

In 1967 the Pittsburgh Penguins (let's just admit it, it's a stupid name) joined the NHL. They were so excited they bought a new mascot, a penguin named Pete. A trainer was hired to teach Pete to skate, but just as Pete was making progress he died of pneumonia. A team named the Penguins and a penguin dying of pneumonia—no wonder it's sometimes hard to take this game seriously.

Now That's a Slapshot

How did an NHL puck end up in space? The answer lies with Canadian astronaut Marc Garneau, who took it with him on his voyage. You can see this famous puck in the Hockey Hall of Fame in downtown Toronto.

Retired Jerseys

When a great player retires from the game, his team jersey number is often retired with him in commemoration. Here is a bit of trivia that will stump your guy.

Can you name the players who had their numbers retired from teams they didn't even play for?

The answer is tricky. It was J.C. Tremblay and Johnny McKenzie. In 1972 Tremblay played for the Montreal Canadiens; he then moved to the WHA's (now disbanded) Quebec Nordiques. Tremblay retired just before the Nordiques moved into the NHL. A few months later, the NHL Nordiques retired his number even though he had technically never played for their NHL team. The situation was similar for McKenzie. During his WHA days, he played for the New England Whalers. When the Whalers became the Hartford Whalers, McKenzie's number was retired, though he didn't play for them.

Stanley Lore

Here's a few tid-bits of trivia, about your hockey guy's holy grail, the Stanley Cup.

The names of all the winning teams are recorded on the silver bands of the Cup. Or are they? One ring is missing. It's the one with the names of the 1929–30 Boston Bruins players engraved on it. No one knows for sure what happened or where it went, but there are strong suspicions that the Bruins' arch rivals, the Montreal Canadiens, had the ring melted down and turned into a small trophy for their coach in 1968.

> **Bruce:** A vicious rumor, probably started by loose Edmonton fans!

Unique among professional sports trophies, the Stanley Cup engraves the names of every player of every champion team (including coaches, owners, and club presidents) on the pedestal. Are there any women's names on the Cup?

Yes, There are several: Sonia Scurfield, Marie Denise DeBartolo York, Marg Norris, and Denise and Marian Ilitch. (To find out why their names were engraved on the Cup, see Chapter 7.)

> **Will:** Hey, I resent that, I can't help it if your heros are thieving hooligans who would deface a hockey icon.

I'm Not a Hockey Player, I Just Play One on TV

Everyone loves hockey, and the proof is in Hollywood. Many actors have played hockey players. John Wayne was a forward in the 1937 film *Idol of the Crowds*. What is more manly than John Wayne and hockey? Ryan O'Neal played for a Harvard team in *Love Story*, and Paul Newman was a minor-league coach and player in *Slap Shot*. Newman even skated for some of the on-ice shots. And we can't forget Rob Lowe in the 1980s film *Youngblood*. I spent hours mastering the rewind button, just to catch Lowe's bare butt in that movie.

Some of hockey's famous Hollywood fans include Susan Sarandon, Goldie Hawn, Cheryl Tiegs, Michael J. Fox, Christopher Reeve, Mike Meyers, and Matthew Perry.

Fun Things to Do with Your Hockey Guy

Now that you know so much about hockey and are officially a fan, hockey will add a new dimension to your love life. Here are a few new fun activities both you and your guy will enjoy.

Hockey Cards

Hockey cards are fun to collect, and every hockey guy loves them. You and your guy can collect and trade them. Choosing what you trade for is fun in itself (nudge, nudge, wink, wink).

Hockey cards also make a fun gift idea. You could make a hockey bouquet for your hockey honey. To make a bouquet, go to your local florist and buy a bunch of flowers, chop the heads off and save them for yourself, attach the hockey cards to the stems with poster putty (the putty used to attach posters to the wall without leaving marks). The putty will make the cards easy to remove from the stems and not damage the cards. See! Martha Stewart has nothing on me.

Enter a Hockey Pool

I thought a hockey playoff pool would be boring when a friend suggested it, but Bruce and I entered. You picked players and earned points according to their playoff performance. The entry with the most points at the end of the playoffs won. With Bruce having the advantage of long-time hockey knowledge, I decided to do a little research on the Internet before entering. I spent a couple hours reading boring team stats and reviews, but I came up with a darn good entry. Being in the pool gave me a reason to really care about the first few rounds of the playoffs. It also gave me a reason to tease Bruce if his players weren't doing well, if I was beating him in the pool (if he was beating me, I called him names). Every day we updated our score sheets, and we never missed a playoff game. It was fun (even though I lost and Bruce is a stinky jerk).

Make Your Own Stanley Cup

Fans can do some very creative things to celebrate the Stanley Cup. During one playoff game, I saw a woman in the stands who had braided her long hair, wove it up onto the top of her head in a Cup shape, and sprayed it silver. If you are a silversmith, you can grab a hunk of silver and hammer out your own Cup. If you are not that talented, then you can pull a Martha Stewart and make a Stanley Cup out of an old bowl (paint it and set it on a painted cake pan). During the Cup finals, you can either drown your sorrows together with your hockey guy by filling it with beer, or share a champagne bath if your team wins.

Have Hockey Parties

Invite your friends over for hockey parties to watch the game or meet the group at a sports bar. You can even have your friends over for a game of road hockey. It's quality bonding time. Besides, when else do you have the chance to hip-check your guy in public?

Rock on, Sister!
Women's Hockey Comes of Age

The women's game and how it's played, with artistry and finesse, could become the role model by which the men should really play the game.

— *Murray Costello, President of the Canadian Amateur Hockey Association, during the 1990 Women's World Championship*

Now that you know how the boys do it, it's time to see how us girls handle the game. We don't have to just watch the boys play anymore, we can watch the girls too. Though it has been an uphill battle, women's hockey has become an international sport of which we can be proud.

Estrogen on Ice

Women's hockey is not a new sport. Far from it. The women's game has been around for more than 100 years, and there was time during the 1920s and 1930s when it was more or less on par with the men's game, both in the number of players and in the number of fans.

The first record of organized women's hockey dates to 1892, when the *Ottawa Citizen* gave a brief summary of a game, identifying the women simply as "Team Number One" and "Team Number Two." (Although the town of Barrie, Ontario often claims to be the birthplace of women's hockey, the game in Ottawa predates it.) The women's game caught on quickly, and within a year it was being played as far away as Alaska.

The Mother of Women's Hockey, so to speak, was the high-flying, high-spirited daughter of Lord Stanley himself: the lovely Lady Isobel. In fact, the first "action shot" of hockey is one of women playing, with Isobel in a white dress swooping toward the puck.

The Golden Years

It is a myth that progress is linear. Things move forward not in a straight line, but in fits and starts, receding and advancing, rising and falling. The single greatest era in women's hockey was in the 1920s, a Golden Age of freedom and fun that all but died soon after. In the 1920s, women's sports were in bloom and teams were popping up all over. Since one of the first jobs available to young woman outside of nursing and teaching was that of telephone operator, many of the best players of the 1920s were phone company employees.

Nice Girls Don't Do It

In 1933, *Chatelaine* magazine urged its readers: "Women Shouldn't Do It!" "It" being sports, in particular, hockey and lacrosse. The *Chatelaine* columnist, a man by the name of Andy Lytle, bemoaned "the sight of leathery-legged, flat-chested girls in sweaters and shorts" running around.

The response was immediate. Women athletes rebuked the magazine's "old-fashioned" ideas. Women's hockey had arrived. Newspapers regularly reported their games, thousands of fans turned out, and the top players became celebrities.

Unfortunately, the 1930s would prove to be the peak. After that, the sport went into a long, drastic decline. First the Depression, then the war, then the stifling neo-conservative values of the 1950s—all conspired to keep women off of the ice and in the kitchen.

The NHL, meanwhile, had solidified its control on professional hockey, and everything from farm leagues to arena times were reserved for men. In many ways, the decline of women's hockey is also the decline of amateur hockey. The big leagues and big money had arrived, and sports reporters and sponsors were flocking to it. The level of hockey undoubtedly improved because of this, but something was lost—or very nearly lost—along the way.

The Lean Years

Although women's hockey suffered through a four-decade drought, the game was still played by stubborn enthusiasts. But socially and financially, support for the game tumbled. It was a long time recuperating. The first stirrings came during the 1960s with the Women's Liberation Movement. In 1967, Lila Ribson and her husband, Harold, pioneers in promoting women's hockey, organized a three-day Lipstick Tournament for women's hockey, which—despite the condescending name—is often cited as a turning point. Women's hockey struggled on for years afterwards, slowly gaining recognition and respect, but the Lipstick Tournament was the first move toward reestablishing women's hockey as a legitimate sport.

Not that everyone welcomed the change. The year of the Lipstick Tournament, a local sports writer complained, "Girls, girls, girls—who needs them? Certainly not the sport of hockey. And yet these feline pretenders seem determined to take over every last vestige of the once proud male domain."

The same sportswriter also made a prediction: "No matter how far one looks into the future, it is unlikely that the gals will ever triumph." Proving him wrong has been one of the great joys of women's hockey over the last thirty years. It took a long time, but "the gals" have indeed triumphed.

Title IX

In the United States, a breakthrough came in 1972, with the passage of Title IX legislation of the Education Amendment. Title IX granted women equal opportunity to sports in any institution receiving any kind of federal funding—which is to say, virtually every high school and college in America. The U.S. Congress, in effect, had outlawed discrimination in sports on the basis of gender. No persons could be excluded from access or participation solely because of their sex.

Title IX guaranteed equal opportunity to athletes, and although—thanks to a loophole—girls were still largely prohibited from playing contact sports, the effects were far-reaching, not only in hockey, but in all areas of sport. In colleges, the number of women playing on varsity teams jumped dramatically between 1972 and 1995, from 2 percent of the total to 33 percent.

North of the border, it was another story. In Canada, the necessary changes in attitude and legislation would take much longer and be fought much harder than in the United States. It would take several high-profile lawsuits and angry counter-suits throughout the 1970s and 1980s before women's rights in sports would be acknowledged.

The Battle for Equal Access

The first shots in the hockey "War of the Sexes" were fired in 1955 by an eight-year-old girl who didn't want to lead a crusade. She just wanted to play hockey. Her name was Abigail Hoffman. Abigail played hockey with her brothers, but there was very little ice time or opportunities for girls to play. So she cut her hair and, registering under the ambiguous name of "Abby," joined an all-boys league in Toronto. No one thought to check her gender. At that age, boys and girls are on equal footing physically; it is only around age thirteen or fourteen, when puberty sets in, that the discrepancy between men and women becomes apparent.

Ab Hoffman went on to become a top defenseman, and was even named to the all-star team, which is when the truth came out. Ironically enough, when it was discovered she was a girl, Abby Hoffman became an immediate media star. It was tough. Under the constant glare of a media spotlight and facing open hostility from the coaches and fellow players, Abby Hoffman became disillusioned and left hockey entirely. She went on to a stellar career in track and swimming, competing in two Olympic Games, and was later named the director of Sports Canada.

In the 1982 Canadian women's hockey championship, the trophy was named the Hoffman Cup, and it now sits proudly in the Hockey Hall of Fame. "I thought you had to be dead to have a trophy named after you," joked Hoffman when it came time to present it.

Gail Cummings

Ironically, teams in the 1950s were far more tolerant than those of the 1970s. When an eleven-year-old goalie named Gail Cummings joined a boys' team in Huntsville, Ontario, in 1977 she sparked a controversy that would reach all the way to the Supreme Court. Gail was a talented player, winning several games and shutting out the boys several times. But Ontario's minor-league hockey association refused to let her continue. The president of the Ontario Minor Hockey Association (OMHA), a

Neanderthal named Al, said he was against "mixing sexes." He didn't think girls should be playing hockey at all.

A provincial human rights hearing overturned the ban against Gail, but the OMHA refused to accept the verdict. They appealed the decision, and the Ontario Supreme Court surprised everyone by overturning the earlier ruling. The OMHA was permitted to ban girls from playing. (Once, during a tournament in the United States, a team from Kitchener, Ontario, left the ice and forfeited the game when they learned the Americans had a girl in net.)

Ultimately, Gail Cummings lost the right to play with her team. She switched to lacrosse and won a top scholarship to play—where else?—in the United States. But the battle continued. In Manitoba, a male coach challenged a similar ban against one of his star players, a girl named Heather Kramble. When he played her anyway, he was suspended and barred from coaching.

Ontario went even further, and in 1982 the province passed an amendment into their human rights code that forbade women from making suits against male-run sports associations. That's right, Ontario became the only province in Canada with explicit segregationist legislation. It was worse than in the days of Queen Victoria. Unfortunately for the dinosaurs in Ontario sport, Canada had just introduced a Charter of Rights and Freedoms that made discrimination based on gender illegal. It was all very confusing and contradictory.

Women on Air

Although the Lipstick Tournament is often cited as such, the first true glimmerings of a renaissance in woman's hockey came in the West. In the mid-1970s, a dominant woman's team, the Edmonton Chimos, made a name for themselves and were soon traveling from town to town, challenging male teams.

Still, it is a sign of what a long, uphill battle women's hockey has had to fight that the first live play-by-play of a women's hockey game didn't occur until 1975, International Women's Year. On November 22 of that year, announcer Dwight McCauley of CJRB Radio in rural Manitoba broadcast live coverage of a match between two local women's teams. Twenty-four years later, women's hockey would be an Olympic sport, broadcast to millions of viewers around the world.

The Ontario Women's Hockey Association (OWHA)

That same year, 1975, also saw the birth of the Ontario Women's Hockey Association. Led by Fran Rider, a tireless promoter of women's hockey, the OWHA was the first and only sports organization of its kind: one solely dedicated to the women's game. The OWHA blazed the way with a women's championship in 1982, which led to an unofficial world's championship and—eventually—to Olympic recognition. Ironically, in a controversial decision, the OWHA had actually *opposed* allowing girls to play on boys' teams for fear that all the best players would decamp.

Justine Blainey

The final battle in Canada was not won until 1987, when a twelve-year-old hockey player named Justine Blainey challenged the earlier Ontario segregation amendment. Fran Rider and the OWHA, surprisingly, were among Justine's harshest opponents. It took four years, $150,000 in legal fees, an appeal to the Supreme Court of Canada, and all kinds of nasty abuse from angry fans and parents, but Justine eventually won her case.

From Abby Hoffman to Justine Blainey it had taken more than thirty years. All these girls wanted to do was play hockey, a game that they loved. That the courts and legislature would throw everything they could against them is quite remarkable—and sad.

Playing with the Boys

So why did these girls want to play with boys in the first place? Three main reasons were given: (1) a lack of competitive girls' teams, (2) a lack of ice time for girls, and (3) better coaching and more games available for boys' teams. Often, the only choice available was a boys' team.

Usually, when they hit puberty, girls stop playing with the boys (at least on ice). It becomes awkward in the dressing room and, more importantly, body-checking—which is never permitted at any level of female hockey—is allowed among boys' teams once the players turn fourteen. A few female players continue on anyway, mainly as goaltenders, where their flexibility and agility are a definite asset. Today, with the boom in women's hockey, there are more and more all-girl teams, and fewer players have to skate with the boys—though some still prefer to. In Canada there are roughly 1,000 girls playing on boys' teams, and the controversy has all but died out. Still, as peewees, several stars of today were forced to cut their hair and disguise their gender: Stephanie O'Sullivan played as "Steve" and Kelly O'Leary played as "Kevin."

Resistance

The good news? Acceptance of female hockey players—both on boys' teams and in their own leagues—is growing. As surveys have shown, support breaks down by age and gender, with the strongest opposition coming from males over age fifty, who still insist, doggedly, that "girls shouldn't play hockey." The younger Gen-X crowd has very little problem with girls and women playing hockey, or any other sport for that matter. So the future looks bright.

The bad news? Women still have to fight for financial support and decent ice times. In hockey-strong areas, women's hockey is often seen as an intrusion, one that robs young boys of opportunities that might take them to the NHL.

The resentment toward women's hockey on a local, arena-to-arena level remains one of the biggest obstacles facing female hockey players. They have the recognition, they have the coverage, they even have the beginning of high-profile heroes and role models. They have a growing, enthusiastic pool of younger players.

All they need now is the ice time at local arenas and the financial support of colleges and sports associations.

From the Anemic '80s to the Robust '90s

During the 1980s, the emphasis for women was on fitness, not sports. Women were meant to be thin and desirable, not athletic and healthy, and the wraithlike anorexic look was all the rage. (Think of Olivia Newton John in her Spandex tights, singing "Let's Get Physical.") Fortunately, this soon evolved into a more robust, active role for women. The 1990s have been the Age of Women's Sports, when women's teams in various fields have finally come into their own.

The Transformation

In a poignant and touching essay on her days playing hockey with a girls' team (dubbed "Betty's Bruisers"), writer Karen Lange remembers the transformation that occurred as she prepared to take to the ice:

> Wriggling into the shoulder pads and pulling on the padded shorts, buckling on the kneepads and jamming my head into the helmet, it was almost as if I was putting on a bigger, bulkier personality, one that did not fear getting hurt or hurting others, one that was allowed to be tough ...

Elizabeth Etue and Megan K. Williams made a similar point in their book on women's hockey, *On the Edge*:

> Playing hockey can be mystical: it can transform ordinary individuals into winged warriors. In hockey, the metamorphosis begins in the dressing room, where you armour yourself with full-body padding that renders you larger than life, virtually invincible. Next, you step into black leather boots with steel blades. Finally, you secure a helmet and face mask on your head to complete the warrior attire. You then glide onto the frozen water, moving faster than seems humanly possible, flying on ice ...

The 1987 World Championship

Women have been playing hockey internationally since at least 1916, when a tournament in Cleveland, Ohio, featured American and Canadian teams going head to head. But for the most part it was restricted to a few border-hopping games.

In 1987, however, six countries—Canada, the United States, Sweden, Switzerland, Holland, and Japan—met for the first Women's World Hockey Championship. Ontario also sent a team, and the final match came down to Team Canada and Ontario. Because the tournament wasn't officially sanctioned by the International Ice Hockey Federation (IIHF), it has been dubbed the "unofficial" first championship. No matter, *Sports Illustrated* and the *New York Times* covered the event, and several countries and organizations sent delegates to watch and take note.

As Marion Coveny, captain of the Ontario team, stepped onto the ice at the start, she said, quietly, "One giant step for womankind."

Hot Pink

In many ways, 1990 was the Year of Women's Hockey. Teams from eight countries met in Ottawa to fight for the first *official* Women's World Ice Hockey Championship. Canada, the United States, and Finland were the dominant countries, but Sweden, Switzerland, Norway, Germany, and Japan all sent teams as well. The 1990 championship had a huge impact. In Canada alone, registration among female hockey players jumped 75 percent, an unprecedented surge.

One of the most controversial decisions Team Canada made at the 1990 championship was to outfit its players in hot-pink uniforms with satiny white shorts. The *Ottawa Citizen* described the outfits as "the wussiest uniforms you've ever seen." The players themselves were nonplussed. Some thought they were kind of hip, in an outrageous sort of way. Others saw them as hopelessly out-of-date and stereotypical; several complained they were simply "too girlie."

Sports writer Jane O'Hara put it best: "Real women don't wear pink. Pink does not inspire fear. Pink does not spark aggression. When you think about battling it out in the corners, you do not think pink. As a team colour, pink stinks."

Fans got into the spirit of things nonetheless, and soon pink pom-poms, pink streamers, pink bow-ties, and pink ribbons were everywhere. Even the Zamboni driver was decked out like a giant pink flamingo.

Fuchsia pink or not, Team Canada steamrolled its way to an easy victory. There was a wide discrepancy of skill between the various countries and at times the games were embarrassingly lopsided. How much fun could the Canadians take in beating the Japanese 18-0? Overall, Team Canada outshot its opponents by a ridiculous margin of 176-23. No one could have predicted then that just eight years later Team Canada would be toppled from its position on the hockey throne.

Still, the glimmer was there, and everyone could see just how much potential the women's game had. *Sports Illustrated*, that bastion of testosterone-induced writing, came out solidly on the side of the women players. "Women's hockey is not the pajama party you might imagine," they assured their readers. "They know how to play the game. Their breakout plays are the same ones used in the NHL, their passes are short and crisp, their skating strong and their puckhandling skills extraordinary."

Women's Hockey Goes Global

The final match in 1990 came down to Canada and the United States, and in a heart-stopping come-from-behind win, Canada captured the gold. In 1990, body-checking was allowed, but with the wide discrepancy in talent, body size, and ability among players and teams, body-checking was banned in 1992 in all future international tournaments, including the Olympics. Today, the "no intentional body-checking" rule is the only official difference between men's and women's hockey.

Etue and Williams see the ban as a positive aspect of the women's game. "The decision [to eliminate intentional body-checking] helped the game immensely: fewer injuries resulted, players were forced to be more creative and the image of the game improved."

The next championship was held in 1992 in Finland, and again the gold-medal contest came down to Canada versus the United States. This time around, however, the match wasn't even close. Canada trounced the U.S. by a score of 8 to 0, but the level of play overall had improved drastically. The International Olympic Committee was impressed, and a few months later they announced that women's hockey would be a part of the 1998 Winter Olympics in Nagano, Japan.

In the meantime, Canada kept winning world tournaments, taking the gold medal in 1994 and again in 1997. On the surface, Canada was a colossus, the bully of women's hockey. But in fact, it was getting harder and harder to beat the Americans. The Finns were stronger than ever, and even China was giving Canada a run for their money. In 1997, the final against the United States went into overtime and Canada barely squeaked out a victory. And as the 1998 Olympics were to prove, the U.S. was now a serious contender.

"Killer" Miller

In 1998, Team Canada was led by Shannon "Killer" Miller, a tough-talking beat cop from Calgary who became the first professional (i.e., fully paid) woman coach in hockey history. Shannon trained her players hard, six days a week, with two hours of ice time a day, together with weight training and cardiovascular workouts. Shannon drives a sleek sports car and has a style all her own. When *Chatelaine* asked her about her penchant for dressing in black, she replied, "It's slimming, intimidating and kind of classy."

Shannon Miller first met a young colt named Hayley Wickenheiser in 1990. Hayley was a talented but impatient twelve-year-old, but Shannon saw promise and talent. Both women were originally from Saskatchewan, but had settled in Calgary. Shannon worked closely with Hayley and her efforts paid off. (She likened training Hayley to "taming a wild horse.") Hayley is one of the best players in the game today, and Shannon Miller is recognized as one of the great coaches of the game.

The Noose Tightens

From 1990 to 1997, Canada won every single Worlds Championship in women's hockey: four tournaments, four finals, four gold-medal victories. And every time, it came down to a Canada–U.S. showdown. But heading into the Nagano Olympics, the two countries were virtually neck and neck in exhibition games.

The rivalry was intense, and often quite barbed—if not always good-natured. During one tournament played on Canadian ice, every time a U.S. player delivered what the fans thought was a cheap shot, the loudspeaker would blare out the Guess Who rock anthem "American woman, stay away from me! American woman, just let me be!"

All of which set the stage for a monumental showdown at the 1998 Winter Olympics, and the pressure was on. The *Ottawa Citizen* declared that, with women competing for the first time and the NHL-stacked Dream Team representing the men, "anything less than two gold medals [at Nagano] will have Canadians crying in their *sake* in the middle of the night."

"Canada has to win the gold medal," wrote columnist Roy MacGregor. Anything less would be "a loss of identity."

What followed was a shock to the system. In a stunning upset on February 17, 1998, a hard-working U.S. team defeated the Canadians to take the first-ever Olympic gold medal in women's hockey, with a solid 3-1 victory. Canada finished with a silver, Finland with the bronze. The loss to the Americans shook the world of Canadian hockey. Just as shocking, the overhyped men's Dream Team of NHL pros fared even worse, managing only a bronze. Incredibly, Canada has not won a gold medal in men's hockey since 1952! (The U.S., meanwhile, has won twice since then, once in 1960 and again in 1980.)

The American women's outstanding showing at Nagano established the United States once and for all as equal players in the Game. Although the U.S. had never defeated Canada in any hockey tournament prior to the '98 Olympics, they had slowly been gaining ground. As one of the American players noted in 1997, "We don't want to waste [our energy] on the little one. We're saving it for the big one." That is, the Olympics.

Sportswriters called their gold medal "Miracle on Ice II," but this was no fluke and it certainly wasn't a miracle. They earned it through skill and relentless play. It was good for the game as well. In fact, considering how important the American market is, the U.S. gold medal was probably the best thing that could have happened to women's hockey in general. Even better, now that women's hockey has full Olympic status, teams are eligible for Olympic grants and special funding from national agencies.

Next up, Salt Lake City in the year 2002. Look for a rematch between Canada and the United States, but don't count out the Finns, or the Swedes, or the Russians, or the Czechs, or even the Chinese. Women's hockey is about to go global.

The Critics

The women's game, of course, has its critics. Some sportswriters have argued that it was too soon for women's hockey to become an Olympic event, that there was too much disparity in talent, that the move was simply a politically correct gesture meant to increase the presence of women at the Olympics.

"Why are we prematurely legitimizing women's hockey?" asked *Toronto Star* sports columnist Rosie DiManno in 1997. DiManno argued that "women's hockey is too embryonic outside of North America, and too unskilled in execution, even here, to justify the Olympic embrace." In DiManno's opinion, opening up women's hockey to full-scale world competition—and letting weaker teams get clobbered in the process—can only be bad for the evolution of the sport. DiManno has since been proved wrong, but her concerns were legitimate.

Many people felt that the early mismatches would only hurt the game by discouraging fledgling nations when their teams were humiliated. In fact, the Olympics electrified fans and boosted interest across the board. It was the carrot that helped inspire all kinds of programs in countries across the world. Simply put, the Winter Olympics were a lifeline for women's hockey.

Far from being premature, the decision to include women's hockey in the Winter Olympics was a long time in coming. It had taken more than twenty years of lobbying to get it on the agenda, and more than 100 years since Isobel Stanley first strapped on a pair of skates and went after a puck.

Women's versus Men's Hockey

Body-checking has always been an issue in women's hockey. As early as 1922, editorials were denouncing physical contact in the women's game. The *Toronto Daily Star* said, somewhat huffily, "If ladies hockey is to be made a success, body checking must be eliminated."

There was some talk after the 1997 championships about reintroducing body-checks to women's hockey, but the motion was defeated. The exclusion of that type of physical contact is the only real difference between men and women's hockey, as far as the rules go. Hockey is a physically punishing game—players collide, slash, block shots, and elbow their way between defenders—regardless of gender.

Body-checking aside, many people argue that if you love hockey, you love hockey. It doesn't matter whether men are playing or women—if it's good, it's good. Even Don Cherry, the sports curmudgeon who is slightly to the right of Ronald Reagan, admires the women's game.

Author David Adams Richards, a fan of both men's and women's hockey, was struck more by the similarity of the two styles rather than by the differences. In both he found a common spirit, a passion, a sense of freedom. For Richards, "sport is sport—and a great athlete, whoever he or she is, is a great athlete."

However, when Karen Kay, a former coach of the U.S. National Team who has worked with both male and female players, was interviewed in *Too Many Men on the Ice*, she made the following observation: "As much as everyone wants to say, 'it's hockey, it's the same thing,' it's not … I think with the women you spend a lot more time trying to build up their confidence because a lot of them aren't as confident as they should be."

Women's hockey doesn't have the speed or bulk that male players bring to the game, and fights are very rare (though they do happen). This doesn't necessarily make women's hockey second-rate. In some ways, it makes it better. When body-checking was disallowed, players were forced to concentrate on strategy and puckhandling. You couldn't simply knock someone over to steal the puck or break up a play. It made the women's game more precise, a game of strategy over power, a game where team play and execution take precedence over raw momentum.

For many fans, what makes women's hockey different is also what makes it better.

In the words of Avery and Stevens, "women have something more to offer—hockey the way it should be—graceful, precise and fast." Etue and Williams agree: "For parents and fans who dislike the goon mentality promoted in the media, women's hockey is a refreshing alternative."

In the conclusion of *Proud Past, Bright Future*, Brian McFarlane writes:

Size and strength may be important factors in basketball and football, but in hockey they are both overrated, especially in women's hockey, which, unlike the men's game, is devoid of goons and enforcers. Stickhandling and passing skills are more important than strength, and small players with a low centre of gravity are often much better skaters than tall, strong players. What women lack in strength, some athletes contend, they make up for in endurance and toughness.

Are Women Purer than Men?

One notion you come across often in interviews with players and coaches is that the women's game is somehow "purer" than the men's because there is no NHL to look forward to. Women can't make a career out of playing hockey. They can't get rich or famous, and thus they play for nobler reasons than do men; in other words, they play for the love of the sport.

Chatelaine went even further in its praise: "Women's hockey is a different game, focusing on speed, skill, skating, shooting and passing, not big goons and NHL crybabies."

I was aghast when I read this. NHL crybabies??? Tell that to Mark "the Moose" Messier and see how far you get. Personally, I find the whole "women's hockey players as purer than men" idea disturbing on two counts. First, I think it's an insult to men. You don't think Wayne Gretzky loves hockey? You don't think the boys struggling in the minors have a passion for the game? And, second, this argument is condescending to women, and defeatist. The fact that women can't make a decent living out of the sport they love is something that needs to be changed, not celebrated. I long for the day when the top women hockey players compete just as fiercely as do men, when they can earn top dollars as a reward for their talent, training, and determination.

As star female player Cammi Granato put it, "Pro hockey players have it good. They make a great living and get to spend the off-season with their families." And what could be better than that?

Going Pro

Women's hockey enthusiasts are hopeful that the 1998 Nagano Olympics will have the same long-term beneficial effect that the 1996 Atlanta Summer Olympics had on women's basketball. The Atlanta Olympics, sometimes dubbed "the Women's Games," helped inspire a professional women's basketball league. With sponsors like Revlon and the backing of the NHL itself, women's hockey has proven itself commercially viable. Sure enough, in 1998, there were rumors of a pro women's hockey league. So far, nothing tangible has come of it, but the promise is in the air and the feeling is one of mounting excitement.

Mind you, not everyone understood the main point of this: that a pro league would give women the respect they deserve. As one patronizing sportswriter gushed, a women's pro league "could include teams like the Montreal Canadiennes and the Colorado Rockettes."

The Future's So Bright, I Gotta Wear Shades

Over the last ten years, male hockey registration in Canada has increased by 13 percent. Female registration has increased 250 percent. In the United States, the rate is even higher, with a 260 percent increase of female hockey registration over the last five years alone. This increase in women's hockey represents the highest shift ever recorded for any organized sport.

After years of playing with ill-fitting skates and awkward equipment designed for men, after slogging through dismal ice times and trekking to distant arenas to play at two in the morning, women's hockey is finally being taken seriously. It is no longer a novelty act; it is a legitimate sport.

There are now more than 37,000 women and girls playing hockey in Canada and the number is increasing exponentially. By the year 2000, the number is expected to reach 150,000. In the United States, the number will reach 74,000 by the year 2000. This is more than a trend. It's an explosion.

The Ringette Connection

Traditionally, female hockey players came from the ranks of dissatisfied figure skaters and talented ringette players. Ringette is a stick-and-ring game that was marketed as a female alternative to hockey. Ringette had a short, sudden boom in the 1980s but has since gone into decline. Women don't need a substitute for hockey anymore.

Figure skating, with its elements of dance and frilly costumes, doesn't appeal to a lot of athletes. Defenseman Vicki Movsessian of the U.S. Olympic team began her sports career as a figure skater but soon changed to hockey. "My personality was too gritty for those outfits they had me wearing," she noted wryly. Or as one young hockey player put it, "I hated figure skating. People figure skating, they hardly wear anything. They're cold."

Body Armor

In case you hadn't noticed, men's bodies and women's bodies are built differently. Although this simple physiological detail is a source of endless interest to men, the fact that women also required different protection was ignored for years by equipment manufacturers. With the exception of the unfortunately named "Lady's Beaver" (the first hockey skate designed specifically for women), women were forced to either use men's ill-fitting equipment or improvise. Proper chest protectors didn't exist, so players sewed cotton pads together and filled them with sawdust, an innovation that apparently began in Prince Edward Island.

In the early 1970s, Tony Marmo, coach of the Massport Jets, a girls' hockey team based in Massachusetts, was frustrated at the lack of quality equipment for female players and he set out to design and make his own line. They included plastic reinforced cups to protect the breasts, and a protective pad to replace the jock strap and cup that boys use. This rigged-up equipment provided important protection, but it was limited to the Massport region.

Not long after, manufacturers finally began producing equipment for women, including chest protectors and skates with narrower widths and better ankle support. Women's ankles tend to be thinner and more prone to spraining than men's. The ankle bones are also further forward in women, giving us a slightly different sense of balance. Our hips also give us a lower center of gravity, none of which is addressed in men's equip-

ment. Fortunately, these concerns are finally being met, and manufacturers have even introduced a "jill strap," which acts in much the same way a jock strap does and provides protection for the pubic bone.

Work with me, Baby! Work with me!

Here's another item from the boy-have-the-times-changed files. As a teenager, young vibrant Cassie Campbell had two interests: hockey and fashion modeling. She would often run directly from hockey practice to a photo shoot, but when she began showing up with bruises on her legs and cuts on her face, the agency was disgusted. "That's it," they said, laying down the law. "If you want to continue modeling, you have to give up hockey." "Fine," said Cassie, and she gave up modeling instead. She went on to a silver medal with Team Canada, after which, of course, the modeling agencies came crawling back.

Cammi Granato

Cammi Granato has been playing hockey since she was five, when she would bat pucks around with her brother Tony (who was later drafted by the NHL). As a child, Cammi had assumed she could play in the big leagues too. She remembers the horrible feeling she had when her mother took her aside in junior high and explained to her that, because she was a girl, she would never be allowed to play for the Chicago Blackhawks (her favorite team). Hockey was only for boys, her mother said, and Cammi cried and cried. "I loved hockey just as much as the boys did," she recalls. Although her NHL dream was obliterated, Cammi stayed in hockey and soon made a name for herself.

Cammi is one of the smartest players skating today. She combines speed and playmaking with precision shooting, and it has earned her accolades. As Team U.S.A.'s all-time leading scorer, with sixty-four points over thirty games, Cammi was awarded the title of U.S.A. Hockey's Woman's Player of the Year in 1996. Considered the best women's player in the United States, and one of the best in the world, Cammi was among the top five scorers in the 1998 Olympics and was instrumental in spearheading the American drive for gold.

Following the triumph of the U.S. team at Nagano, Cammi Granato hit the talk-show circuit, appearing with fellow players on everything from MTV to CNN, from "Late Night with David Letterman" to "Regis and Kathie Lee." The real height of fame arrived, however, when the U.S. Women's Team appeared on the front of a Wheaties box. It was then that women's hockey had truly come into its own.

Hayley "Wicked" Wickenheiser

Hayley Wickenheiser (a distant cousin of Doug Wickenheiser, a number one NHL draft pick), has been hailed as the best all-round women's hockey player in the world. She is fiercely competitive. She has a hot temper and, on at least one occasion, has dropped her gloves and "popped" an opposing player in the head—though "popped" is a pretty mild word for the action of a player as tall and strong as Hayley, who at 5'9" and 170 pounds, was one of the biggest players on the Canadian team. Authors Elizabeth Etue and Megan K. Williams describe Hayley as "a firecracker on ice, explosive and greedy with the puck."

At Nagano, Hayley tied Cammi Granato with eight points in six games (though with fewer total goals and more assists than Cammi). Young, energetic, and remarkably focused, Hayley is the player to watch. The tired old cliché "the Wayne Gretzky of women's hockey" may seem a bit lame at this point, but in Hayley's case it applies.

In many ways, Hayley's fire-wagon style of play is reminiscent of an earlier child protégé, Angela James, the star of the 1990 World Championship and a player who had also been dubbed "the Wayne Gretzky of women's hockey."

Hayley was only eleven years old when that first championship was held, and she was in awe of Angela. In many ways, Angela James helped inspire Hayley Wickenheiser. Just four years later, at the ripe old age of fifteen, Hayley tried out for Team Canada—and made it, proving herself a key player in the 1994 championship when she played alongside Angela.

Angela scored two spectacular goals in the gold-medal game and was named the game's MVP. Sadly, she was later cut from Canada's Olympic team just prior to the 1998 Games.

Hayley, meanwhile, was invited by Philadelphia Flyer's GM Bobby Clarke to their 1998 training camp. In an interview with *Hockey News*, Hayley is quoted as saying that, although she got a lot out of the camp and enjoyed the challenge and opportunity immensely, she has no designs on playing in the NHL itself. "For women," she said, "the Olympics are our NHL." And Hayley is already focused on Salt Lake in 2002.

Drop
the
Gloves
Drop
the
Gloves
Drop
the
Gloves
Drop
the
Gloves
Drop
the

Kelly Dyer

The first woman to play pro hockey in a men's league was goalie Kelly Dyer of Massachusetts. Kelly had been playing hockey since the age of eleven, when her idol was Bobby Orr of the Boston Bruins. The Boston area was hockey crazy, and Kelly often got pulled into games, everything from street hockey to organized rink bouts. She had a stellar collegiate career in net and played for Team U.S.A. in the first official Women's Championship in 1990. She remembers the excitement well; kids would follow her down the street, asking for autographs.

In 1993, she received an unexpected phone call from a minor-league pro men's team. She played first for Jacksonville and was then traded to a team in West Palm Beach. When she arrived she found herself the center of a media circus. This was at around the same time that another female goalie, Manon Rheaume of Canada, was making headlines of her own at an NHL training camp in Tampa Bay (see below).

Kelly was thrown right into the thick of things as the starting goalie in her first game—and she was credited with her first win. She was a solid goaltender, playing nine games, with a 8-1 record, including one victory in sudden-death overtime. The West Palm Beach team won the divisional championship in 1994 and 1995 with Kelly on their roster. Unfortunately, business problems helped end Kelly's career; the team she was playing with was sold, renamed, and driven into bankruptcy. Still, Kelly credits her eighteen months as a pro with teaching her more about hockey than her previous fifteen years in the game.

Although she missed the chemistry and close bonding that she felt with women's teams, she got on well with the other players in West Palm Beach. "They were like my brothers," she says, echoing a sentiment common among female players playing with men. (It is surprising how many female hockey players came from families with athletic, rough-and-tumble brothers.)

Kelly has since retired from active play and is developing a line of hockey equipment specially designed for women. According to her, women play a "smarter" game of hockey, one that is more European in style, where the emphasis is on playmaking rather than showboating, where the players work together with a stronger work ethic than among men. Indeed, the problem is sometimes the other extreme; women tend to pass instead of shoot and at times can play too cautiously, too methodically. Dyer laughingly remembers one of her early coaches in women's hockey screaming at the players, "Don't be afraid to score the goal! That's the whole point of the game." Kelly's own motto is worth remembering as well: "Don't tell me what I can't do."

Manon Rheaume

Kelly Dyer is not the only woman to play on a professional men's team. Erin Whitten, a top women's goalie, was the first woman ever to record a win in pro hockey when she played briefly in a male league. (No female forward or defenseman has yet played on a men's pro team.)

But the highest-profile player of all is Manon Rheaume, dubbed "The First Lady of Hockey." Manon grew up north of Quebec City, where her father was a hockey coach. In 1991, she became the first woman ever to play in a major junior game. During play she took a hard slapshot to the head, which split her helmet and opened a gash above her eye. She continued playing, but when the ref noticed the blood he stopped play and Manon was forced out. She received stitches and a bruised forehead for her efforts. As it turns out, the coach on the opposing team had told his players to shoot high and at her head to scare her.

In 1992, Manon backstopped Canada to a victory at the Women's World Championship in Finland, and was invited for a try-out with the Tampa Bay Lightning. The NHL. The Big League.

Although decried by some as staging a publicity stunt, Phil Esposito, the team director at Tampa Bay, didn't realize Manon was a woman at first. His scout, Jacques Campeau, showed Phil a clip of Manon in action in the men's junior league and asked him what he thought.

"Well," said Phil. "He's a little small for a goalie, but he moves well. He has good reflexes. We can invite him to camp." Jacques then informed him that the goalie in question was a woman. Phil, to his credit, didn't blink. "Well, let's see what she's got." Of the eight goalies invited to training camp, Manon had the third-best goals-against average.

And on September 23, 1992, Manon Rheaume made hockey history when she became the first woman to play in an NHL game. She was in goal for the first period in an opening-round exhibition match between Tampa Bay and St. Louis. She did well for a rookie goaltender under relentless scrutiny; she stopped seven shots and let in two. When the period ended, she skated off to a standing ovation. Not only was she the first woman to play in an NHL game, she was the first woman ever to play in any of the Big Four pro sports (baseball, football, basketball, and hockey).

Time called her "the Seventh Wonder of the Sports World." She was invited to appear on David Letterman's show, pursued by paparazzi, hounded by fans, and—at the age of twenty-one—had become an instant celebrity. *Playboy* offered her $40,000 (a number sometimes reported as $75,000) to pose in the nude, but she refused. "Not for a million dollars," she said.

Bruce:
Will, I'd pay you not to pose nude.

Teena:
Hey, Manon wasn't the first NHL player to get an offer like that. Mark Messier once posed bare-chested and sweaty for sportswriter Christie Blatchford as a "Sunshine Boy."

Will:
What!! Is she crazy? I'd pose nude for a million dollars. Heck, I'd do it for a lot less.

Will:
Eww.

Manon Rheaume, for all the hype and glitz, is a dedicated, hard-working goalie who has spent years fine-tuning her craft. She was also very lucky. As Manon herself cheerfully admits, "I was in the right place at the right time, with the right people in my corner. Born under the right sign, perhaps." And although there has been some resentment among other female players, who work just as hard as Manon but without the fame or money, for the most part everyone understands what a golden opportunity it was for her. Here was a chance to train and play with the best players and the best coaches available. How could she pass that up?

In her memoir, *Manon: Alone in the Front of the Net*, she asks "If you were given an opportunity to reach for the stars, would you walk away?"

Manon hasn't given up on woman's hockey either. In the 1998 Olympics she joined Team Canada along with goalie Lesley Reddon. In the words of Kelly Dyer, Manon Rheaume "is a unique individual, a classy lady."

Tomorrow's Stars

It's been a hell of a ride. From woolen skirts to hot pink to Olympic status. But the strongest image I have of women's hockey is not the gold-medal game between Canada and the United States or the hype that surrounded Manon's NHL debut. No. The strongest image I have is of the ecstatic mob of young fans who swarmed around Team Canada captain and silver-medalist Stacy Wilson when she returned to her home province of New Brunswick after the 1998 Olympics. Stacy was surrounded; she signed autographs, shook hands and looked tired, surprised, exhilarated.

A grade-six girl had come to welcome home her hero, and she summed up everything we need to know about women's hockey and where it's going: "I love watching hockey," she said, beaming. "And everything makes me want to play."

Women's hockey has come of age. Young girls are now having hockey dreams of their own.

In Conversation with Thérèse Brisson

Thérèse is a veteran defensewoman, although she prefers the term "defender" or simply "defense." ("Why," she asks, "is a forward simply a forward and a goalie a goalie, but a defense is defined by gender?")

Thérèse Brisson: The Stats

> Height: 5'7"
> Born: October 6, 1966
> Weight: 150 pounds
> Position: Defense, shoots right
> Number: 6

Hockey Background

- Female Rookie of the Year (1987) and Female Athlete of the Year (1988 and 1989) while playing at Concordia University
- Inducted into Concordia University Sports Hall of Fame in April 1997
- 1993 Quebec Provincial Champion with Ferlands 4-Glaces, Most Valuable Defence of the Championship
- 1994 and the 1995 Women's Senior National Hockey Champions, Team Quebec, named Most Valuable Defence of Championship (1995)
- 1996 Bronze Medal at the National Championships with the New Brunswick Maritime Sports Blades

National Team Involvement

- Team Canada member at the U.S. Olympic Festival in 1993 in San Antonio, Texas
- Member of the Gold Medal team at the 1994 World Championship in Lake Placid, New York
- Member of the Gold-Medal team at the 1996 Pacific Rim in Richmond, British Columbia
- Member of the Gold-Medal team at the 1996 3-Nations Cup in Ottawa, Ontario
- Member of the Gold-Medal team at the 1997 World Championship in Kitchener, Ontario
- Named to the 1998 Olympic team on December 9, 1997
- Member of the Silver-Medal team at the 1998 Olympic Games in Nagano, Japan (five goals and two assists in six games)
- Captain of the Gold-Medal team at the 1999 Women's World Championships.

All in the Family

Thérèse Brisson came from a large family, one brother and three sisters. Her whole family was involved in sports (and still is). Her brother, Michael, is a swimmer and her sisters, Susan, Cathy, and Tara, all played ringette and still play recreational hockey.

Thérèse played ringette as a young girl; her father even coached some of the earlier teams that she was involved in. It was through ringette that she was introduced to hockey. Little did she know that this was the beginning of the path that would lead her to many championships, to a place on the first women's Olympic hockey team, and eventually, to become a role model for all young girls with a hockey dream.

From Ringette to Nagano: An Interview

In talking with Thérèse, a few themes emerge: the importance of creating female role models within the sport, the importance of developing a better varsity development program for women's hockey, and the natural transition which has occurred from ringette to hockey.

Girlfriend's Guide: Let's start with the obvious. How did you first get involved in hockey?

Thérèse Brisson: Well, I grew up in Montreal, and back in the late 1970s and early 1980s the big sport out there—in the West Island anyway—was ringette. I played ringette from an early age, but in grade seven I became involved in hockey. We were really lucky at the school I went to. One of our teachers, an English teacher named Frank Miller, organized a girls' hockey team for girls age twelve to seventeen. Recognizing that ringette was really the main activity, he would collect our ringette schedule and plan a hockey program around it. We used to play the college teams and university teams, and we went to two tournaments in Ontario. Frank Miller really did this singlehandedly, without very much support from the school administrators. Unfortunately, without financial support from the school, the program eventually died, and they haven't had a girls' high school program there since.

GG: Was ringette your favorite sport?

TB: I loved ringette. The club development was quite advanced at that time. We would go to nationals every year and there would be 500 athletes there. I was playing ringette when I was six, and hockey when I was twelve.

GG: Were you always defense?

TB: No, I was a forward. I was a winger in ringette. It was at Concordia University that I was moved to defense. I was at tryouts the first year—I was trying for center or forward—and the coach, Julie Healy, watched me for a while and said, "Well, I think you are going to be defense. [She laughs.] I remember being horror-struck.

GG: And you've played defense ever since?

TB: That's right.

GG: One of the problems that a lot of female players face is a lack of ice time and a lack of opportunity. Did you have trouble with that?

TB: I was lucky because of the ringette. I could skate twenty hours a week if I wanted to. It was fun because we would have hockey practice right after school, and we would have ringette that night. I also got involved in coaching and refereeing. So I never experienced a problem. I know a lot of the girls who come up playing hockey have had real trouble with getting ice time.

GG: Who were your heroes? As an offensive defense, I would guess Bobby Orr or Paul Coffey.

TB: No, no. As a matter of fact, I would say I had no role models in hockey. I just didn't identify with them. The NHL wasn't something I could be or do, so why would I identity with Bobby Orr or Paul Coffey? My heroes were athletes like [track and field star] Diane Jones-Konihowski. I remember watching Diane at the Montreal Olympics in 1976 and screaming at the TV. It was great. The female athletes were the ones I identified with because that was someone— someone I could be. Why would I identify with male players?

GG: The reason I asked you about your early role models is that things seemed to have shifted dramatically. Today, you are a role model for young girls who want to play hockey. Is this going to make a big difference?

TB: I hope so. Have you seen that Esso commercial, where the girls are playing hockey and they're imagining themselves as hockey stars— female hockey stars?

GG: I know, I love that commercial! I get goosebumps whenever I watch it.

TB: I think that commercial defines the change in thinking that has occurred in hockey now that young players *have* heroes and *have* role models. There are a lot of young kids now breaking into the program. I was reading a sports publication the other day, and they were asking a young player about who her role models were and she said Thérèse Brisson. I was astounded. I mean, it's funny. I never thought about it, but yes, the young players have it a little easier today.

GG: They have heroes. They have people to look up to, people to emulate.

TB: I think it's great.

GG: You went to Concordia University in Montreal in the Department of Kinesiology, is that right?

TB: Actually, it's the Department of Exercise Science. It's a three-year university program. I did my graduate work, my Masters and my Ph.D., at Université de Montréal.

GG: So you studied in French and in English.

TB: Yes, but my first language is English. I consider myself an anglo-phone. When I graduated from Concordia a woman called me up, France St. Louis, who was organizing the teams in a women's league. France, of course, is one of the star athletes in women's hockey. I was actually the first anglophone to play in that league. France and I became very good friends.

GG: For so many women, for so long, there was no NHL contract wait-ing for them, no promise of a million-dollar contract. It's been said that in many ways women's hockey is better than men's—or at least *purer*. How do you feel about that? Is there any truth to that?

TB: I don't know. I suppose it's the difference between the pursuit of excellence and the pursuit of cash. The older players certainly fought an uphill battle. The women who are just now finishing up their hockey careers—the France St. Louises and the Angela Jameses—they had to build the system. You didn't just show up and play. You had to coach, you had to ref, you had to organize. You really had to make it happen.

GG: Where do you fit in? Do you feel closer to the trail-blazers like France St. Louis, or to the younger players, the Hayley Wickenheisers who are just now coming into their own?

TB: [She laughs] Oh, I'm one of the Old Guard, I suppose.

GG: Another point that comes up is the lack of body-checking in women's hockey. Some people argue that this forces women to be more creative in their playmaking. As a defense player, what is your feeling about body-checking? Wouldn't it make your job a lot easier if you could simply knock the opposing players down and steal the puck?

TB: To tell you the truth, I don't notice a whole lot of difference in the game. In women's hockey, we *are* allowed body contact. We are allowed to pin someone on the boards, we can ride the check out. The only thing we can't do is lower our shoulder, take two steps, and hit someone center ice. That's the only real tangible difference. Now, I think if you look at a junior boys' hockey game, where all they do is wind up and clean each other out, then you would see a remarkable difference in how the game is played. But at the Olympics, I didn't notice a huge difference between the men's game and the women's. Sure, the men are bigger, they shoot the puck harder than we do and they can move a bit faster, but as far as the flow of the game, the way the puck is moved—I don't see a big difference.

GG: As a university professor do you still have time to actually play the game?

TB: It's very hard right now, because I'm still trying to be an athlete and I don't have the time to run around being an administrator, coach, official. There's a danger in getting caught up in that. I have maybe a year or two left with the national team.

GG: Really? How old are you now?

TB: I'm thirty-one.

GG: I didn't realize that the shelf life of athletes was so short. France St. Louis played on the Olympic team at age thirty-nine, and she was still going strong last time I looked. Do you think you'll make it to Salt Lake in 2002?

TB: Oh, I don't know if I'd want to. I think in two years I'll have a decision to make whether I'd like to make another run or not. My initial reaction is, probably not. It's a lot of work. The national team, the Olympic team: they talk a lot about the privilege and the honor of being involved—and it is a privilege—but it's also a big responsibility. And in a way, when the Old Guard retires it opens up positions for younger players coming up, which is good for the sport.

GG: Is there a lot of good young talent coming up?

TB: I'd say we're about ten years behind the Americans in our seventeen-to-twenty-four age group. And that's because they have a very well-developed system in the universities and colleges, which supports women's sports. Whereas here, our varsity system is terrible. It's pathetic. It really is. UNB is a prime example: they had a club team here for a while, but there is no funding. They won't put up funding for a woman's team. And that's fairly typical, especially in the Atlantic region. There are a few programs I would consider leaders, Concordia being one, the University of Toronto being another, York and Guelph, and out West as well. But the big problem, as far as Canadian woman's hockey goes, is a lack of funding and support on the varsity level. We don't have the development taking place at that age group that we should have.

GG: I'm surprised and a little shocked. I would have thought that UNB, having such a high-profile player such as yourself on the faculty—an Olympic medalist and one of the top defense players in the world—I would have thought they would have a thriving women's hockey program.

TB: Unfortunately, that has nothing to do with it. It comes down to university funding, and the support simply isn't there. It's a shame. There are some really strong players here. If they had a fully funded program, they could have at least one Olympic team player coming out of this university.

GG: Is the real problem at the government level, or the university level?

TB: At the university level. The money isn't available, and in the eyes of many, athletics isn't a real priority.

GG: What do you think are the prospects for a professional women's league?

TB: We may see something after Salt Lake. I would be scared to see something before then, because I don't think we have the depth yet. The main thing we have to concentrate on is developing young players at a school level, before we start looking to a pro league. If we want to stay competitive [in Canada] we have to develop the varsity programs more. Down south in the U.S. they are far more advanced.

GG: You were a member of the 1994 gold-medal team at Lake Placid. Was that your first international competition?

TB: I was involved in the development program for new players in 1993, which went to San Antonio. Actually, I had first tried out for the national team at the Quebec level, and I kind of made a mess out of it. I was invited to the training camp for the 1990 World's Championship, but I didn't go. Partly, because they were asking for quite a bit of money and I was a grad student at the time and I didn't have it. They wanted $300 to go to the camp, and I was playing ringette competitively then, and I was going to a world's championship in ringette that year as well. So I decided not to go to the 1990 World's.

GG: You were spared the hot-pink uniforms.

TB: I was spared the hot-pink uniforms. I did go to watch the final, and I remember thinking, "Oh, I made a terrible mistake." And I think it hurt me later on when I went to the camp in 1992. I didn't make the first cut, which was quite disappointing. It was partly because I wasn't viewed as being a "serious" player.

GG: Because you had turned down the 1990 invitation?

TB: That's right. So Lake Placid was my first World's. I didn't get to go to Finland in '92.

GG: How important were the Olympics for women's hockey? Has the impact been exaggerated?

TB: The attitude toward women's hockey completely changed when it became part of the Olympic Games. When I went to the World's in 1994, I had just finished my Masters, and I was starting my Ph.D.

"spare the hot pink uniforms"

and I was also working at Concordia as a part-time faculty. I was never there, and I was getting myself into hot water. There was this attitude of "What are you doing? Why are you wasting your time?" They were kind of turning their noses up at it. So I played at the World's and that was fine, but once it was announced that women's hockey would be an Olympic sport [the announcement was made just a few months after the World's] everything changed. All of sudden, it became a legitimate pursuit. It was really quite remarkable, because for me it was still the same setting. I was still going to Université de Montréal, same supervisor, same personnel I was working among, but suddenly what I was doing was acceptable. I was finally recognized as a serious athlete.

GG: Did the pressure increase? Comparing Lake Placid World's with the Olympics, did it get harder?

TB: I would say it got easier.

GG: Well, you certainly did well at Nagano. You were eighth overall in points, which is excellent for defense.

TB: I had a good Games. I set some very specific goals for myself and I worked toward them. I was lucky as well, because I wasn't one of the high-profile players so I didn't have the media scrutiny or the pressure on me. I was able to just focus on playing.

GG: Are you satisfied with your performance at the Olympics?

TB: Well, in something like the Olympics there is the event and the experience. The experience was wonderful, it was everything I expected—and I had high expectations. I told myself that this was probably my first and last Olympics, and it was amazing. With the event, however, I was disappointed.

GG: Why? Most people would be quite happy to win a silver medal.

TB: [Smiling tightly] We didn't play our best on the night when it mattered most. Personally, I am satisfied. I am happy with my performance, but I don't think we played our best as a team.

GG: How about Killer Miller? Was she as tough a coach as they say?

TB: I think Shannon Miller did the best job she could in the circumstances. She is very focused. You have to be prepared to follow her lead and fulfill your role. Coaching is so important.

GG: Do you need to be a woman to coach women's hockey?

TB: No, not at all. But coaching a woman's team is different from coaching men's. I think women are more concerned with team goals, where men are more concerned with individual goals. I know, I play with the guys a lot and let me tell you, some of the things they say to each other on the bench … [She laughs and shakes her head.] There is no way you would hear women talking like that to each other. I think women's hockey is more of a team sport.

GG: Is there life after hockey?

TB: Well, you come to a point in your athletic career where you have to accept that you aren't going to make a living out of playing hockey and you have to start thinking about other things. [She laughs.] I'll be up for tenure in two years, so …

CONCLUSION

So now girlfriend, I crown you a Hockey Fan, a Hockey Chick, a Hockey Babe. You know all you need to know to understand the game and why your guy (and girlfriends) love it. If your thirst for hockey knowledge is still not quenched or if you want to know even more than your Hockey Guy, here is a list of further resources:

The Hockey Hall of Fame—www.hof.com—More than you will ever want to know about the game.

National Hockey Players Association—www.nhlpa.com—See all the cuties here!

National Hockey League Home Page—www.nhl.com— Find team sites here, and live game radio.

Hockey Night in Canada—www.hockey.cbc.ca—Lots of hockey news, up to the minute scores, and video clips of Coaches Corner with Don Cherry- like we want to see him again!

The Hockey News Online—www.thn.com—CNN *Sports Illustrated*— www.cnnsi.com—Online magazines with hockey news, read it before your guy does.

Andria Hunter's Home Page—www.whockey.com—A wonderful site all about women's hockey by a former member of Canada's national team.